THE HISTORY & FOLKLORE OF *American Country Tinware 1700-1900*

THE HISTORY & FOLKLORE OF

Apple tray. Courtesy of The
Henry Ford Museum,
Dearborn, Michigan.

American Country Tinware 1700-1900

Margaret Coffin

Galahad Books • New York City

Published by Galahad Books, a division of A & W
Promotional Book Corporation, 95 Madison Avenue,
New York, N.Y. 10016, by arrangement with Thomas
Nelson & Sons.

Library of Congress Catalog Card No.: 73-88482
ISBN: 0–88365–126–2

Manufactured in the United States of America.

*Dedicated to
Chuck
and the boys*

Table of Contents

Introduction 11

A Dictionary of Tinware Shapes 21

Early Tinsmithing in Massachusetts 35

Apprentices, Toolmakers, Decorators,
and Peddlers in Connecticut 49

The Stevenses of Stevens Plains, Maine;
Other Maine Smiths and Peddlers 89

Spread of the Tin Industry to New York
and Vermont 107

Tinmen and Peddlers in Pennsylvania and
Further West 147

Leaves from the Journals of a Smith, a
Peddler, and a Tinker 169

Peddler Folklore 185

Identification and Care of Old
Tinware 203

Glossary 211

Bibliography 212

Appendix I 216

Appendix II 217

Index 220

Introduction

$\mathcal{D}$URING THE twentieth century, American tinware, neglected by earlier antiquarians who cherished wrought iron, copper, brass, pewter, and silver, has come into its own. Today folks collect it, reproduce it, paint it, investigate its history, and start family feuds over who will inherit Aunt Jennifer's painted sugar bowl.

Abe Veeder of Scotia, New York, was the first tinware collector of whom I have heard. He was a queer fellow, who, at the end of the nineteenth century and beginning of the twentieth, maintained a private historical museum of sorts which he called the Old Fort. Abe bought, begged, borrowed, and reclaimed tinware of any kind he could find, but finally, impoverished, he was reduced to patching his roof with trays and making a bonfire beneath a heap of tin utensils in order to melt and collect solder to sell. Abe's tin pile, the size of a small haystack, was a landmark near the Mohawk River in the early 1900s.

Like colored glassware or Staffordshire pottery, tinware, especially when varnished with japan paint and stenciled or decorated with oils, becomes a collector's delight because it makes a handsome display. One collector has built corner shelves for his tinware, the center of interest in his living room; another uses a plate rail along a paneled wall for a showcase. Some of my collection is in an open pine cupboard; more is on floor-to-ceiling shelves that my husband built to accommodate my hobby. A decorated caddy on a mantel or a coffee table becomes a conversation piece; a tray and candleholders, a coffeepot or box filled with flowers makes an unusual ornament for table or buffet.

Unpainted tinware, which used to be "poor man's silver," has a homely charm which just fits today with old cherry, pine, and maple furniture. The American ware, painted or unpainted, belongs with crewel and homespun, jacquard-woven coverlets, cross-stitched samplers, hooked or braided rugs, and blown glass.

POPULARITY OF TINWARE IN EARLIER DAYS

American housewives in colonial days also approved highly of these tin utensils first made here during the early part of the eighteenth century. Although a few pieces of tinware were listed in seventeenth-century inventories, these pieces were probably brought here from Europe; and even there, the manufacture of tinplate was, at best, only haphazard until the 1700s. (Except for his clothes, the total effects of Jan Verbeek who died in New York in 1693 included: a Bible; two "writing books"; a bed, bolster, and two pillows; two blankets, one foot cloth; a closet; a tool chest; a clothes chest; a table and bench; a kettle; and-irons, tongs, trammel; a small iron pot; a platter and two plates; a great rocking chair and another chair; a green coverlet; and *a tin can*.)

All of the first pieces of tinware were unpainted, and the light, bright, and inexpensive kitchen utensils enjoyed a popularity easy to understand. Before their time womenfolk had struggled with iron pots and unwholesome wooden trenchers, clumsy and difficult to clean. In the households of some of the well-to-do, copper and brass wares were used, but these were expensive, in constant need of scouring, and sometimes toxic. Pewter, which contained lead, could not stand direct heat and was exceedingly soft. (Today's pewter with a lower lead content is much more practical.) Decorated tinware, which came into vogue in the beginning of the nineteenth century, added color, less plentiful in the households of the early 1800s than in the modern home, and helped to satisfy the housewife's esthetic sense. These bright designs on tinware, often characteristic of specific tin centers, appeal to today's collectors and add significance to the tinware collection.

A TINSMITH'S MATERIALS

The tinsmith made his ware from tinplate, which is iron or steel pressed thin at a rolling mill, then cleaned and dipped in molten tin at a plating works. The sheet is dipped several times, the actual number of dippings determined by the thickness of tin desired. Early sheets of tinplate were ten by fourteen inches. (Trays were once designated as quarter-sheet, half-sheet, or full-sheet size.) Besides tinplate, wire and solder were the smith's chief materials although eventually he came to use rivets, patent ears for buckets, drawer-pull handles for boxes, and pewter finials for the lids of coffeepots or teapots.

In 1645-1646 John Winthrop spearheaded the building of an iron-works in Saugus, Massachusetts Bay Colony. This early, short-lived industry produced as much as a ton of cast iron a day. Although the American colonists knew of other deposits of iron ore, such as the one worked by William Byrd of Virginia, and constructed several iron-works for smelting, they were prohibited by England—jealously guarding her own industries—from rolling sheet metal. Anyway, tin itself was not discovered in the United States until the nineteenth century. Because of the absence of raw tin and of rolling mills, for years the tinplate used by American smiths was brought to this country from Great Britain where the tin mines which burrow into the Cornish coast are still active. A typical shipment was advertised in *The New-York Gazette and Weekly Mercury*, May 3, 1773:

> James Morton has received per the Grace, Chambers Captain, from Bristol, and from the New Diana, Wilson Captain, from Liverpool; for sale at store, Tin Plates and Wire.

Although the American tinplate industry was born in about 1830, American tinmen continued to import plate from Britain's plentiful supply until 1890 when the McKinley Tariff Act made this impractical.

TOOLS AND TECHNIQUES

Making tinware was a relatively easy process. The tools of the first tinsmith were simple: wooden mallets, tin shears or snips of varying sizes, chisels, a soldering iron. Working on a wooden bench, he used a charcoal brazier to heat his soldering iron and melt his solder. His patterns were tinplate templates, and after sections of utensils had been cut, he soldered them together. Seams were sometimes first hooked over each other, then hammered tight. Outside edges were usually rolled over wire for added strength, although occasionally they were merely doubled over. If a piece of tinware required curved sections, these were shaped over a carefully whittled wooden form, an anvil, or an iron stake driven into the workbench. These stakes were of vari-

AVAILABILITY OF ANTIQUE TINWARE TODAY

ous sizes and shapes; one might form a fish horn, another a coffeepot spout, another a scoop.

There is still antique tinware to be found: decorated and undecorated. Attics are being cleaned out, collections dispersed, auctions held to settle estates. Because antiquarians have a new respect for tinware, pieces which a few years ago might have been thrown out are being saved. Recently an acquaintance of mine rescued a rare gallery tray from beneath draining milk cans. When a friend allowed me to search through the miscellany left as junk in the home of a deceased relative, I found a decorated shaker on a shelf behind the attic door and a painted snuffer tray in a scrap of silk among remnants of clothing.

The most likely place to find tinware, though, is in your favorite antique shop. If you are looking for a particular item, ask a dealer to help you find it. And, if you have friends who haunt the antique shops and white elephant and rummage sales set them looking for your collectible along with their own. The outdoor flea markets which have become popular in the United States in recent years and the antique shows which draw dealers together from all directions also prove sometimes to be gold mines for treasure hunters. (Perhaps, though, only the dedicated can claim that the thrill of the search surmounts the ache of tired feet and the feeling of claustrophobia caused by the crowds at shows such as the excellent ones held in New York's Coliseum or the Westchester Civic Center in White Plains, New York.) Although sometimes prices at the big shows seem astronomical, there are also bargains. I still covet the food safe that I saw at a New York show priced at several hundred dollars, but, at the same exhibition, I bought two pierced panels from another safe for three dollars.

Dyed-in-the-wool antiquers have discovered that a number of dealers have congregated in certain communities: in Fitzwilliam, New Hampshire; Sheffield, Massachusetts; Dania, Florida; and Rock City Falls, New York, for instance, where fifteen dealers have taken over an old mansion. My antiquing expeditions in search of tinware and furniture for an old farmhouse in the Adirondacks have covered thousands of miles —from shops in Tampa's Spanishtown to Harry Knapp's emporium in Rutland, Vermont. Have you ever tried to carry an old accountant's desk in a Volkswagen? A large pie safe in a small house trailer? A butcher table on top of a car in a high wind?

Country auctions are exciting if you can find ones that are genuine. Avoid the "salted" sales where the tire tracks of vans are still fresh behind the house. Don't be surprised, though, if auction prices of popular items go higher than the tags in local antique shops. If you are in a tourist area during "the season," beware. Some sales are arranged to amuse vacationers and the quality of goods for sale is poor.

After only a few antiquing tours or visits to auctions or flea markets, even the novice begins to feel knowledgeable. This may well be an exciting new way to spend time (as well as money). And the collector will discover that the investment is wise: a good antique never becomes secondhand, and its value will increase, not decrease, as time passes. The person who loves and knows antiques seems also to acquire a special awareness of and feeling for history.

This volume is largely the result of pure cussedness. When, years ago, someone suggested that there wasn't much material about the old-time tinsmiths, peddlers, and decorators, a persistent nagging urged me to find out for myself. I suspected that somewhere, if one dug deep enough, there was information to find.

As a child I had learned to respect our heritage when my history-loving mother led me from one of the museums she enjoyed to another. And, I learned then, too, to take advantage of my story-telling relatives. Grandfather Mattison told tales of his oil-field days in Pennsylvania where he and his partner leased the property *next to* John D. Rockefeller. There were stories galore as well about Grandpa Fuller, a Civil War veteran whose leg was amputated after the Battle of Winchester while he lay on a church door holding a bullet between his teeth. The peg leg Grandpa wore afterward became a convenient signal for my dad during his courting days—he always knew when Grandfather was coming! Then there were the reminiscences about Great-great-uncle Richard Thomas who married a witch—but that's another story.

My interest in the techniques of early tray and furniture decoration and the encouragement of fellow members of the Historical Society of Early American Decoration, an organization dedicated to the study and practice of old-time decoration and to research in this field, have spurred me on. The sympathetic interest of my husband and my sons (humoring me, perhaps, because until recently I was the only woman in the family) has also been significant.

Miss Dorothy Filley Bidwell and Mr. and Mrs. Marcus Filley have contributed details about their ancestors for which I am grateful. Mrs. Theodore Whitbeck, descendant of the Butlers, has also been more than generous with information. Owners of tinware collections have allowed me the privilege of photographing their pieces; Mr. James Stevens has been especially helpful. Both Dr. Louis Jones and the late Dr. Harold W. Thompson allowed me to study their folklore files.

Photographs, except for those furnished by museums and historical societies, have been taken by my husband and Frank Rollins.

For their very special encouragement, suggestions, and assistance I wish to thank Zilla Lea, Catherine Hutter, and Charles V. S. Borst. Other people who have helped by telling a story, finding an appropriate document, lending a picture, or editing copy, are innumerable. My sincere gratitude goes to all of these, many unnamed, who have added to the *History and Folklore of American Country Tinware 1700-1900.*

The chapters which follow deal with tinsmiths, peddlers, and decorators, often in specific tin centers, such as Stevens Plains, Maine, or Berlin, Connecticut. Usually these tinmen are discussed in the order just suggested, with the historical background first and unique characteristics of decoration at the chapter's end. Some tin centers have added specific contributions to the industry; these are identified in chapter headings.

The folklore of the peddlers has, in some instances, been difficult to identify as such; often fact and folk story have become so entwined they cannot be separated. The tin peddler, though, plays an important role in American legend, and the legends about him are essential in delineating the role of the peddler.

The first eight chapters recount the history and lore of the tinsmith, the tin peddler, and the tinware decorator. The last chapter suggests means of identifying old ware and methods of preserving it. The photographs have been carefully chosen to complement the text.

Happy browsing!

A Dictionary of Tinware Shapes

*T*HE TRADE SIGNS that colonial tinmen hung in front of their shops bore bold replicas of their handiwork: The Sign of the Golden Candlestick, The Sign of the Coffeepot. Julius Mickey of Winston-Salem, North Carolina, marked his mid-nineteenth-century place of business (which still stands) with a model of an eight-foot, curved-spout coffeepot with a conical lid, inside of which a spy is reputed to have hidden during the Civil War.

In early city directories, street names pinpointed the locales where tinmen worked: Tin Pot Alley in New York City, Mechanic's Alley in Baltimore, Brazier's Alley in Philadelphia. And place names identified towns, such as Tinsmith's Locks, Pennsylvania; Tinkerville, New Hampshire; Tinkertown (now Hobart), New York, where tinsmithing must have been of major importance.

TINWARE

Eighteenth- and nineteenth-century smiths made an amazing assortment of ware, and today we speculate about some of the items in their ledgers and inventories. The inelegant "spit box" was probably a cuspidor, but what was the "night hawk" mentioned in the early-nineteenth-century ledger of Thomas Hayward of Woodstock, Connecticut? Was it a lantern? Why is an item worth thirty-one cents identified in the ledger of another smith as an "old maid's teapot"? What is a "drudging box"—a dredging box or flour sifter? (Box seems a strange word to substitute for shaker, but there are frequent references to "pepperboxes." Can we assume that a "sandbox" is not a child's play area but a sprinkler for sand used to blot the ink from a quill pen?

The use of tinplate was so widespread by the 1800s that that period might well be referred to as the Tin Age. Tinplate, which later became important in American industry, was, at first,

Infant's nursing bottle. Courtesy of The Hershey Estates Museum, Hershey, Pennsylvania.

Rare, elaborate cookie cutters (or cake stamps) from the collection of Pennsylvania antiques of Dr. Earl Robaker, White Plains, New York.

used primarily on the farm and in the home to equip the dairy and the kitchen; it was also a favorite material for early lighting devices. Tinned milk pans, milk strainers, milk pails, and dippers were considered necessities by anyone in the country or in the village who kept one or more cows. William Gilbert of Philadelphia advertised: "Wholesale and retail—tin churns, cream cans, tin milk pans. . . ." Tinplate formed the essential unit of the sausage stuffer, which was a part of a farm's standard equipment, and of the equally important contraption the farmer used to smoke out bees when he wanted to gather honey. One type of churn, shaped like a pig with a handle for a tail, was made from tinplate.

No household after 1800 was complete without a supply of tinware. In a chapter entitled "On the Care of Kitchen, Cellar and Storeroom" from *A Treatise of Domestic Economy*, published in 1845, Katherine Beecher lists these utensils as requisites for the bride:

> Bread-pans, large and small pattypans, cake-pans, with a centre tube to insure their baking well, pie-dishes (of block-tin), a covered butter-kettle, covered kettles to hold berries, two sauce-pans, a large oil-can (with a cock), a lamp filler, a lantern, broad-bottomed candlesticks, for the kitchen a candle-box, a funnel or tunnel, a reflector, for baking warm cakes an oven or tin-kitchen, an apple-corer, an apple-roaster, an egg-boiler, two sugar-scoops, and flour and meal-scoop, a set of mugs, three dippers, a pint, quart and gallon measure, a set of scales and weights, three or four pails, painted on the outside, a slop bucket with a tight cover, painted on the outside, a milk-strainer, a gravy-strainer, a colander, a dredging-box, a pepper-box, a large and small grater, a box in which to keep cheese, also a large one for cake, and a still larger one for bread with tight covers.

Squirrel cage. Courtesy of the New York State Historical Association, Cooperstown, New York.

This list of ware made for Duncan Mackarthur, itemized in the mid-nineteenth-century ledger of Henry Brandow of Morrisania, New York, gives us an idea of prices of tinplate items.

1 coal hod	1.00
1 pan	.25
1 chamber pail	1.50
1 water pail	.38
1 sauce pan	.18
1 cake turner	.13
1½ pint dipper	.06
1½ gallon dipper	.18
1 drudging box	.13
1 French skimmer	.31
1 flour sieve	.31
2 10" round pie tins	.25
3 8" round pie tins	.27
1 7" round pie tin	.08
2 dish pans	.75
1 oval pudding pan	.18
1 scoop	.18
1 scoop	.12

Housewives used tin knife-boxes, tin steamers and nutmeg graters, basting ladles and yeast cans, teakettles, jelly kettles, and skimmers. There were tea "steepers" and coffee "boilers" and watering pots, syrup jugs and milk pitchers, pot lids, fenders, and dust pans. Tin boxes held spices, flour, pepper and salt, pills, trinkets, cash, stamps, and gunpowder.

For the gentleman there was a satin-lined oval box to hold his epaulets—if he were a military man—and a shaped tin box to protect his hat. Later boxes were also silk-lined and used for high stiff collars.

Tinsmiths shaped tea trays, bread trays, and apple trays, hand basins and tubs for bathing, cages for squirrels and parrots, and even nursing bottles.

Fancy tin top hats and stiff tin bonnets with the ruching crimped from metal were in vogue for "tin" wedding anniversaries. Such headgear is exhibited at the Henry Ford Museum in Dearborn, Michigan, and at Monroe, New York, at the Old Museum Village. Although there are no identifying details, hats are inventoried along with colanders and lamp fillers in the Connecticut Filley tinshop. (I have also seen framed tin-anniversary wedding certificates.)

Tea set made for tin wedding anniversary. Courtesy of the New York State Historical Association, Cooperstown, New York.

Jointed and painted tin toy. Courtesy of the New York State Historical Association, Cooperstown, New York.

Tin mirror and picture frames were popular, especially in the Southwest. The edges of these were usually scalloped, and pierced and punched patterns provided ornamentation. Frames duplicating those with beveled edges made from solid pine or cherry were also shaped from tin.

Weathervanes were made from cast metals and from all sorts of sheet metal including tinplate. The Missouri Historical Society in St. Louis owns a weathervane, a rooster in silhouette, which was cut by a tinsmith from Boonville, Missouri, in the mid-nineteenth century. Several similar vanes may also be seen at the Shelburne Museum in Vermont.

A July 12, 1817, *Missouri Gazette* carries Reuben Neal's advertisement for manufactured tin- and copperware, listing among other items wash kettles, stew kettles, teakettles, and stills. In *Candleday Art*, Marion Rawson has praise for the old still, and other bits of tinware:

> Even some of the old whiskey stills with their contraptions for coil and tube, make it worth our while to give this humble medium a glance, and there were homemade ear-horns for the "deef," and dinner horns for the hungry with really lovely curves and flourishes, the crude little candle-holders to be somehow balanced on the boughs of the Christmas tree, the tinderbox with its precious load for starting a fire, the quaint tin-kitchens for roasting meat before a flame, tin balls, boxlike toasters, tin bee-traps and an endless chain of strainers, graters, funnels, and "tunnels," of every sort and variety, and all defying the world to find an ugly line in their make-up.

In pre-plastic days and long before the plentiful tin toys many of us remember—those stamped into shape and lithographed in bright colors—infants were playing with tin rattles and older children with tin horns, jointed dolls, and tea

Coffeepot with bold design. Courtesy of the Hershey Estates Museum, Hershey, Pennsylvania.

Deed box with heavy japan paint background. Fine painting resembles signed work of Butler girls. Collection of the author.

Caddy and deed box with borders like those on signed Mercy North tray. Notice the mottled background of the box. Collection of the author.

Hooked or crooked spout coffeepot has its bottom raised by a curved flange. Courtesy of The H. F. DuPont Winterthur Museum, Winterthur, Delaware.

This candleholder with its yellow "rope" border and gay flowers is a rare type. Decoration is typical of Connecticut and Pennsylvania. Courtesy of the Philadelphia Museum of Art, Philadelphia, Pennsylvania.

The design on this japanned coffeepot features large gaudy flowers. Decoration is typical of Pennsylvania. Courtesy of The H. F. DuPont Winterthur Museum, Winterthur, Delaware.

Low oval caddy. Red fruit has yellow paint blended by fingertip. Courtesy of the Hershey Estates Museum, Hershey, Pennsylvania.

Notice the symmetry of the pattern on this coffeepot. Courtesy of the Hershey Estates Museum, Hershey, Pennsylvania.

Sugar bowl in mint condition. Autumn leaves on white band. Courtesy of the Hershey Estates Museum, Hershey, Pennsylvania.

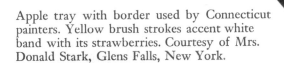

Apple tray with border used by Connecticut painters. Yellow brush strokes accent white band with its strawberries. Courtesy of Mrs. Donald Stark, Glens Falls, New York.

Teapot with rare white-petaled flowers and blue-green leaves. Courtesy of the Hershey Estates Museum, Hershey, Pennsylvania.

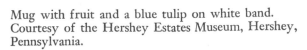

Mug with fruit and a blue tulip on white band. Courtesy of the Hershey Estates Museum, Hershey, Pennsylvania.

Octagonal, cut-corner, or coffin lid tray with
Vermont-New York border painted in typical
country tin colors. Collection of the author.

Caddy marked "Spice" has bright fruit
and leaves. Collection of the author.

Country-painted tray from Maine. Courtesy of
The Historical Society of Early American
Decoration, Inc., Exhibit at The Farmers Museum,
Cooperstown, New York.

Deed or document box with vivid
pattern. Collection of author.

Extra large deed box filled with legal papers was discovered in an attic. Busy pattern. Courtesy of Mrs. A. P. Robertson, Glens Falls, New York.

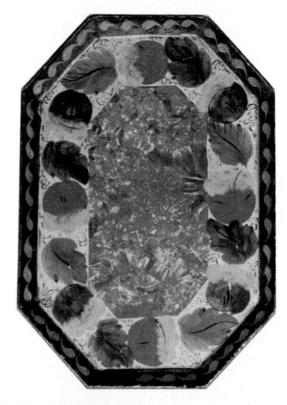

Octagonal tray with crystallized floor is of medium size. Found in Pennsylvania. Collection of the author.

Octagonal tray with "Mary Ellen B——— (illegible) Brookfield 1845" scratched in back. A Maine piece. Collection of the author.

Syrup jug has similar design on both sides. Found in northeastern New York State. Collection of the author.

Low caddy shows the skill of an accomplished decorator. Perhaps from a Filley shop. Collection of the author.

Cream jug resembles syrup jug but has no cover. Found in Pennsylvania. Collection of the author.

Oval box of type some-
times used for epaulets.
Mint condition. Pattern
of kind often found in
New York State. Notice
red stems. Collection
of the author.

Round canister used in
kitchen. White overstrokes
originally on blue almost
worn off. Collection of the
author.

Bun tray was painted by one of the Butler
girls of Greenville, New York. Painting in
Minerva Butler's album at left is similar.
Courtesy of the New York State Historical
Association.

Coffeepot in fine condition has elaborate
pattern on both sides. Found in Connecticut.
Collection of the author.

Deed (or document) box has gay design
of type found frequently in New York
State and Vermont. An unusual feature
is the green brush-stroke border on top.
Collection of the author.

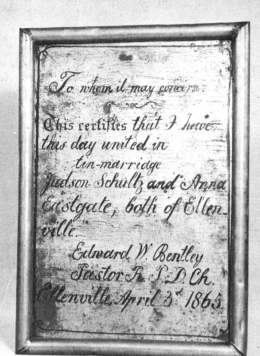

To whom it may concern.

This certifies that I have this day united in tin-marriage Judson Schultz and Anna Eastgate, both of Ellenville.

Edward W. Bentley
Pastor R. I. D. Ch.
Ellenville, April 3rd 1865.

Hat and wedding certificate to commemorate tin wedding anniversary. Courtesy of the Old Museum Village, Monroe, New York.

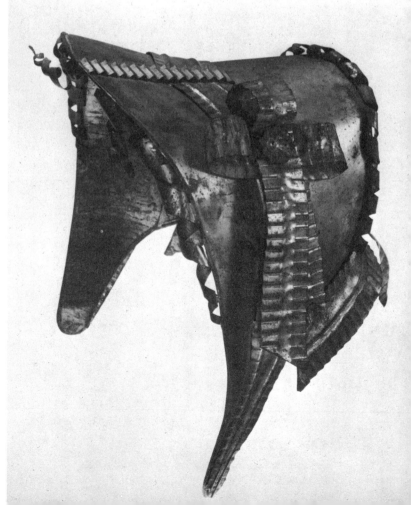

Bonnet made for tin wedding anniversary. Courtesy of The Henry Ford Museum, Dearborn, Michigan.

Child's dainty tea set made by a tinsmith for his niece. Courtesy of Mr. William White, Schenectady, New York.

Cake stand or tazza. Courtesy of Old Sturbridge Village, Sturbridge, Massachusetts.

sets. Fantastic whirligigs waved their arms or legs as the wind blew or as someone pulled a string. Doll-size and child-size tin plates taught the ABC's; symbols were stamped around the outside edge while a portrait, a scene, or a nursery rhyme was centered on the floor of the plate.

Because of the way it can be cut and soldered, sheet tin has been used to make some marvelous,

completely novel pieces. Consider the tin foot one tinsmith made for himself, and the grandfather's clock case which another ambitious tinsmith fabricated for his own pleasure.

Handy foot warmers, carried to church or on long sleigh rides, prevented frozen feet. These boxes had wooden frames with sides and tops of tinplate pierced in elaborate designs. A tray inside held glowing coals. (Even after pot-bellied stoves had been set up in meetinghouses, many foot stoves were carefully preserved. Only a short time ago a varied assortment was found in a storeroom above King's Chapel in Boston, saved by some vestryman who must have suspected that the newfangled furnaces were an impractical notion.)

LIGHTING DEVICES

A study of early lighting in America reveals remarkable ingenuity in lighting devices and in materials burned: rushes soaked in grease; splinters of pitch pine; candles of tallow, bayberry, and spermaceti; wicks dipped in common fish-liver oil as well as whale oil, "whey butter," lard oil, and camphene. Although some of these fixtures were made from copper, brass, silver, pewter, iron, wood, glass, and pottery, tinware fixtures were, because of their low cost, probably most plentiful. The assortment of styles in which they were made was so great that only comparatively few typical devices will be described here.

Betty lamps, the open vessels in which an oil-soaked wick was burned, though frequently made from iron, were occasionally tin, and two such styles are identified today as Ipswich Bettys and Newburyport Bettys. The "table-tidy" upon which a Betty lamp frequently sat was most often tinplate. This aptly-named standard looked like a handled candlestick with a crimped edge saucer on top; it elevated the lamp neatly from the table top and provided a safe means for carrying it.

A contrivance that might have been a handleless teapot resting on a shallow base was really a Cape Cod spout lamp. The excess oil that dripped from the wick hanging from the spout ran down a trough back into the reservoir in the lamp base. (Wicks often absorbed oil faster than it could burn.)

A lamp designed especially for the out-of-doors was in the shape of a teakettle with a half dozen spouts. Another type was fitted on a long stick to be carried in nighttime processions.

Many whale-oil lamps, which ranged in height from a few inches to over a foot, were mere bulbous tanks on top of candlestick bases. These and lamps burning other fuels often had two wicks to increase the amount of light by improving draft and combustion; the two wicks with their brighter light being the discovery of young Ben Franklin when he was apprenticed to his father Josiah, a Boston chandler.

The reservoir of a petticoat lamp sat on a conical skirt which hid a socket to fit the post of a tall-backed chair.

In *Colonial Lighting*, Arthur Hayward labels a horizontal cylindrical lamp with two wicks a guest-room light. A disc of tin over one wick held herbs or spices, allowing the host to scent the air and perhaps offset the odor of burning fish oil.

Multiple tin devices were contrived to fit in specific places or meet special needs. Tiny, versatile peg lamps nestled conveniently in brackets or in the tops of candlesticks. In the magnificent display of lighting devices in the tavern at Old Sturbridge Village, there is a shop light, a simple whale-oil lamp mounted inside a tin pan which reflected the flame.

Tin reflectors were common. They were used with sconces and lanterns as well as with lamps. Some sconces have several concave tin or pewter discs soldered on the back piece in much the same way that bits of mirror were mounted to magnify light. The reflectors of some wall sconces resemble crude pie plates; others are oval, curving gently behind single or double candle sockets. The sconces were simple or ornate, in sizes that varied with their purposes. These were favorite lighting fixtures in churches, courtrooms, and ballrooms as well as in the parlor.

Tinplate candleholders which correspond to twentieth-century floor lamps are ingenious. Bases were apt to be conical and weighted with sand. (Similar lamps for the tabletop were weighted in the same manner.) An iron rod from the base of the four-and-a-half- or five-foot reading light supported a candleholder with from two to five candles. The whole top could be adjusted in height by inserting a pin through the iron support. A shepherd's crook or ring at the top served as a handle.

Other tin candleholders were listed in a smith's inventory as "large and small back," "spring,"

Sponge-cake type candlesticks made by Shaker tinsmiths. Courtesy of the New York State Historical Association, Cooperstown, New York.

"stand-up," and "large and small bottom." There were deep-saucered candleholders like sponge cake pans and minute holders that clipped to books while people read. Some of the large-bottom candleholders may have been pie tins with candle sockets centered in them; other such sockets perched on top of tinder boxes. There were tall candlesticks with no handles and squat holders with handles, the type which sat on the stand at the foot of the stairs, ready for each member of the family at bedtime.

Candle lanterns for use outside were designed to shield the flame yet give off as much light as possible. A popular type of tinplate lantern was described by Longfellow:

Pierced with holes they were, and round,
And roofed like the top of a lighthouse.

This is the kind commonly called the Paul Revere lantern today although it was not actu-

Ingenious Shaker candleholder which clips to book. Collection of the author.

Simple tin chandelier.
Courtesy of Old Sturbridge
Village, Sturbridge,
Massachusetts.

ally the type used to signal "One, if by land—two, if by sea," on the eve of the American Revolution. Other tin lanterns with glass or thin horn on one or more sides gave off extra light. Handles were attached to tops or backs of these outdoor lighting contrivances which were made in all shapes—round, square, rectangular, hexagonal, or semicircular. Tops were usually vented, sometimes with intricate piercing.

Chandeliers of tinplate are still being discovered. Some of these are extremely simple, with only a central cylinder and four arms to hold candles. Fancier fixtures were handmade with tiers of gracefully curved tin straps ending in candle sockets. A circular band of sheet tin might hold as many as a dozen small candleholders soldered in place. This particular chandelier could be suspended from the ceiling by

(Left) Unusual pierced tin lantern. Glass on four sides adds light and shields candle flames. (Right) Sturdy chandelier has metal hoop to support individual candleholders. Courtesy of Old Sturbridge Village, Sturbridge, Massachusetts.

a chain hooked to an iron bail, fastened to the chandelier as if it were a kettle.

Prevalent during the nineteenth century, especially in eastern Pennsylvania and other sections with a large German population, were the minuscule tin clips used to hold miniature candles for Christmas-tree decorations. A particular itinerant Pennsylvania tinker was renowned for the stars he cut to top these festive trees.

Early candles, kept hidden from rodents in tin candle boxes, were made in tin or pewter candle molds and extinguished with tin snuffers shaped like small dunce caps. By the nineteenth century scissors-like snuffers for snipping charred wick were being pressed from tinplate. Many of us can remember the tin container with the potato stuck on the spout which was used when kerosene replaced animal fat and fish oil as a fuel.

Early
Tinsmithing
in Massachusetts

*T*ODAY MASSACHUSETTS—with its painstaking
duplications of an earlier way of life at Old Sturbridge Village and at Old Deerfield; its preservation of more limited facets of American cultural
heritage in museums such as the whaling museum at New Bedford, the Indian museum, the
Shaker cottage, the art gallery, and Fruitlands
at Harvard village; and its multitude of colonial
homes all over the state which have been restored and opened to the public—offers a broad
and valuable education to everyone with an interest in America's past. Old Sturbridge Village
is of particular interest because of its tin peddler's cart; its tin shop and collection of tinsmithing tools; and its exhibition, on the second
floor of the tavern, of lighting devices, many
made from tinplate. In the restored early homes,
antiquarians may see an old tin bake oven ready
for use beside the hearth; a nutmeg grater, whole
nutmegs strewn beside it on an old kitchen
table; lamps set out, ready for wicks to be
cleaned and reservoirs filled. And besides its res-
torations, Massachusetts has especially fine antique shops, another important contribution to
the lover of Americana.

SHEM DROWNE

The grasshopper weathervane on Boston's Fanueil Hall remains a symbol of the excellent craftsmanship of the colonial American artisan. Have you also seen the Indian vane in the museum of the Massachusetts Historical Society? This short-legged, glass-eyed Indian once stood lookout on the old Boston Province House. Both weathercocks were made by Shem Drowne, who was perhaps America's first tin- and coppersmith. Drowne was identified as a smith when, in 1720, he purchased two buildings on one of Boston's crooked cobblestone streets. These may have housed his shop and his family, for Drowne had married in 1712. The real estate sale was noted:

> Northeast of Gibbs' property was a three tenement estate owned by John Barrell. In 1720 he conveyed the two easterly buildings to Shem Drowne, tin-plate-worker.

Drowne's day book in the American Antiquarian Society Library in Worcester, Massachusetts, is a fascinating ledger. It has entries starting in the front in 1720 and continuing until 1723; in the back, entries are dated 1754. The later entries frequently mention Thomas, Shem's son, who seems to have become a partner in his father's business by 1754.

Shem Drowne made tinware in his own shop and sold it from his store. His stock, listed in an inventory as being kept "in the shop, in the closett, in the cock loft, and in the suller," consisted chiefly of tinware, although there were some items, including many of the weathercocks, made of copper and brass. The fact that many workers in sheet metal labeled themselves specifically "tinsmiths" or "coppersmiths" when tax rolls were made up or a census was taken is confusing, until one realizes that, despite this, these smiths were apt to work with all sheet metals.

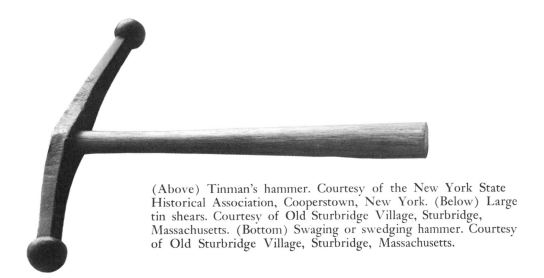

(Above) Tinman's hammer. Courtesy of the New York State Historical Association, Cooperstown, New York. (Below) Large tin shears. Courtesy of Old Sturbridge Village, Sturbridge, Massachusetts. (Bottom) Swaging or swedging hammer. Courtesy of Old Sturbridge Village, Sturbridge, Massachusetts.

If *Drowne's Wooden Image* by Nathaniel Hawthorne is to be believed, Shem was also noted as a wood carver. This makes sense when one remembers how objects such as the fancy weathervanes were made. The malleable sheet metal was shaped by hammering over carved wooden molds into figures as intricate as the grasshopper and the Indian mentioned earlier.

A miscellany of ammunition and hardware was stocked by Drowne to be sold along with the sheet metal products. "Shott," "nales," and "chisells" are among items listed.

The ledger mentions a number of custom orders such as Mrs. Tarrant's parrot cage, which was ordered by Captain Cook at a cost of fourteen shillings. Captain Hendrey bought a "trumpett" for eighteen shillings. (Probably this was an ear trumpet, an eighteenth-century hearing aid.) Ship-captain Plaisted purchased a tin trunk, a water pot, and a "sas" pan. The account of

Stake used to shape tin. Courtesy of Old Sturbridge Village, Sturbridge, Massachusetts.

Tinsmith's charcoal brazier. Courtesy of the New York State Historical Association, Cooperstown, New York.

Samuel Shrimpton shows a tinderbox and a poop light, the latter costing five pounds. Perhaps the "Tin Case for Bottles" was stowed in a ship's locker.

Tinmen were often called upon to be tinkers; the Drownes mended trays, tin ovens, and coffeepots. Shem horned lanterns and even painted a water pot for five shillings, four pence.

Shem Drowne had a wholesale trade as well as a retail one. Richard Harding, a Boston merchant, bought in large quantities; William Mann of Marblehead was a wholesale customer. As many as one hundred "lanthorn" frames at a time were sent to Joseph Temple of Boston, and a long list of ware went to Oxenbridge Thatcher, marked by Drowne "fore him to Sell fore me." A few items from that list follow:

1 dozen puding pans 'Sorted
3 graters
1 dozen Bear [beer?] quart pots
1 dozen lamps

39

3 large culenders
3 small ditto
6 quart funels
1 dozen pepper boxes

Most of Drowne's transactions were for cash although one entry in the last section of the ledger reads "by 12 pounds butter." At another time Shem accepted half a cord of wood in payment for a debt, and when Benjamin Davis settled his account with Thomas Drowne, the debt was paid in tea.

When, in 1730, the spire of Boston's Old South Church was completed, the pastor made a note: "They raised the vane or wethercock, Shem Drowne, tinman, made it." In 1765, the weathervane of the meeting house in Deerfield, Massachusetts, was removed for repairing and regilding, and the bird was fitted with new globe eyes by Shem. One of the other references to weathercocks in Drowne's book notes: "North Meeting House – to make a wethercock – 10 pounds, 7 shillings." This particular vane consisted of an arrow and a hollow ball for records, having as additional ornament a five-pointed star. The six-foot vane weighed one hundred seventeen pounds, and the rector, William Croswell, complained, "It is not so light a matter as weathervanes are supposed to be."

On one of its visits to a repairman, a notation was discovered inside the Faneuil Hall grasshopper:

Shem Drowne made it May 25, 1742. To my brethren and fellow Grasshoppers. Fell in ye year 1753 by my Old Master above. Again like to have met with my Utter Ruin by Fire, but hopping Timely from my Public Scituation, came off with Broken Bones and much Bruised. Cured and fixed. . . . Old Master's son Thomas Drowne June 28, 1768, and though I will promise to Discharge my Office, yet I shall Vary as ye Wind.

Drowne had has finger in more than one pie. He was agent for the Pemaquid Patent, "all of the land of New England lying and being from forty-eight degrees of northerly latitude and in length by all that breadth from Sea to Sea." As Proprietor he encouraged immigrants to settle in the Massachusetts Bay Colony by giving out parcels of land. He was at one time also responsible for the fortifications of Boston and he was a deacon in his church. Throughout his life the tinman was "a man of affairs and activity . . . engaged in many important matters in the early days of Charleston and Boston."

The master smith lived almost a century to die just before the outbreak of the Revolution. On January 13, 1774, a Boston gentleman, Thomas Newell, wrote in his diary:

> Thursday – more moderate weather. Very good sledding; great plenty of provisions and grain. Old Mr. Shem Drowne, ob. AE 91: he was the first tin-plate-worker that ever came to Boston, New England.

The Massachusetts Gazette and the Boston Weekly News Letter of January 20, 1774, recorded his demise with a curt statement:

> Died – Deacon Shem Drowne, aged 91 years. He was a sincere Christian and well-respected among us.

Other tinsmiths were mentioned in Drowne's ledger, so that, although Thomas Newell identified him as Boston's first tinplate worker, by 1720 Shem was not the only such mechanic there. (There are indications that Newell, himself, was a tinsmith.) Presumably John Elliot from whom Drowne borrowed "½ a stone of cours five wier" [seven pounds of coarse number five wire] was a tinsmith. Certainly Richard Esterbrucks, who bought twenty tinplates from

Machine for crimping tin plate. Courtesy of Old Sturbridge Village, Sturbridge, Massachusetts.

PARSONS, WHITING AND THEIR TIN MACHINES

Shem in 1722 must have been a tinman. Also recorded is the loan of twenty-five single tin-plates to Joseph Bradford, tinman. On November 24, 1720, Joseph Miller also purchased one hundred fifty sheets of plate from the Drowne shop.

During the first years of tinsmithing in America, ware was made by hand—manu-factured, in the literal sense of the word. By the end of the eighteenth century tinmen began tinkering with machines to speed up production and meet increasing demands for household ware. Why should each part of each utensil be cut individually with tinsnips? Couldn't there be some device for reinforcing edges mechanically? These and other questions plagued Eli Parsons, a Dedham, Massachusetts, smith.

According to legend, Eli and his bride Abigail were attending services at the First Church in Dedham on the Sabbath. As the preacher reached a fiery climax, Eli roused to jump up shouting, "I've got it! I've got it!" The surprised congregation saw him run from the sanctuary to put his plans for the first tin machine on paper. Soon Parsons and Calvin Whiting of Dedham formed a partnership. On April 14, 1804, they obtained a patent signed by James Madison, Secretary of State, which records this description of the set of machines.

A pair of rolling shears, for cutting sheet tin, a Sweep Gage, used for holding tin plates, while cut into circular forms, also for holding them while the edge is turned to form the bottoms of the vessels; a Machine for turning said edges; a Machine for giving a second turn to the said edges of the bottoms; a Machine for locking the sides and the edges together; a Machine for giving the first turn for wiring; a Machine for giving the second turn for wiring; a Machine for completing the operation of wiring by closing the

Machine for bending edges of tinplate. Courtesy of Old Sturbridge Village, Sturbridge, Massachusetts.

edge around the wire; a Machine for turning the edges of sheets of tin to be united to make larger vessels; and a Machine for locking the edges together after they are turned, and a Machine for burring or turning the lower edges of the vessel to receive the bottom.

Using another important innovation, these machines formed plates, trays, and ladles. The inventors claimed to be the original inventors of the art of making these pieces "by a stamp, at one operation." Before this time ladles, spoons, and similar pieces had been cast in molds or shaped by the blacksmith. Stamping from sheet metal provided a larger quantity of these items at a lower cost. A collection including just these early stamped pieces might prove interesting.

At the Dedham Historical Society Library there are papers in the handwriting of Whiting which discuss one of these early sets of machines called simply "Patent Machine for Working Tin Plate." Mr. Whiting wrote in this paper dated December 14, 1805:

> The publick are respectfully informed, that a machine has recently been invented (by Calvin Whiting and Eli Parsons of Dedham, Commonwealth of Massachusetts) for working Tin Plate, into the various kinds of ware necessary for use, for which a patent is obtained according to law.
>
> The machine is considered by those who have had an opportunity to examine it, to be one of the most useful inventions that ever originated in our country & worthy the attention of every tin plate worker who considers his time of any value. Although it is very simple in its construction and of course can require but little repair yet it facilitates and can save three fourths of the labor necessary in any other mode of working tin plate before practised, and at the same time perform the work in general much neater and more thoroughly than it can be done by hand. It turns, locks and grooves all the seams in a vessel, it turns the seams and completes the operation of wiring by closing the edge around the

wire, forming the vessel at the same time. It cuts bottoms of all sizes, turns and locks the sides and the bottoms together closing them perfectly tight.

The whole machine is calculated to move with a down wheel, which may be put into motion by water, steem, horse, man or any other power. The rollers that perform the different operations above described will make from ninety to one hundred and twenty revolutions in a Minute.

There is an amusing note in Mr. Whiting's instructions for the use of his machinery. "Although the vessel to be made may be cut out by the machinery yet it is found from Experience that by the reason of the multiplicity of gages required to cut the various forms of Vessels it can be but little saving in labour, therefore practise cutting out the bodies of the Vessels from patterns in the usual way." (The usual way was the old-fashioned method of cutting with hand shears.)

During the first decade of the 1800s, Whiting and Parsons opened a shop on Whiting's property. Before long Barnabas Langdon joined the partnership and they advertised:

> Those who incline to purchase the Patent Rights to the above machinery may have opportunity by applying to the Patent Tin Manufactory a little west of the Court House, Dedham, whare Shopkeepers & others may be supplied with any quantity of plain or Jap. and Gilt Tinware at the most reduced prices in the United States.

Smiths bought the machines from the inventors and the right to use the machines in certain specified places.

In 1806, rights for machines had been sold to many smiths in several states and territories. Remember that smiths were apt to live in the North during part of the year and move to the southern states for the rest of the year. The following list probably does not mean that machines had been sold or rights granted to thirty-eight different tinsmiths. Many smiths were granted the right to use their sets of machines in more than one state.

Vermont	2
New Hampshire	2
Massachusetts	5
Rhode Island	2
Connecticut	2
New York	4
New Jersey	2
Delaware	1
Maryland	3
Virginia	5
North Carolina	3
South Carolina	2
Missouri Territory	1
Ohio	2
Indiana Territory including Michigan	2

PEDDLERS

Among the Parsons-Whiting records there is a note from a tin peddler:

1803

Major Whiting Sir –
I have a distant relation, the Bearor of this note who wishes to try his luck at pedling. He is as I suppose a clever fellow but as I have no tin here – any more than I want myself, if you have any tin unsold if you would let him have a load out of your shop I will answer for the same. In so doing you will oblige him and me and perhaps not disoblige yourself.

Vivian B. Yale
Tin Pedlar

The first peddlers, more numerous in Connecticut than in any other area, were really the brave young men of the eighteenth century: the adventurers, and sometimes, the scholars. A Whittier schoolmaster could "doff at ease the scholar's gowns/ To peddle wares from town to town."

Painting of old-time peddler by Edward Lamson Henry (1814-1919). Courtesy of New York State Museum, Albany, New York.

And George Brinley, at about the time of the Civil War, bartered tinware for rare editions stored in attics until he had amassed a collection that became the basis for a famous library.

The peddlers enjoyed their reputation for craftiness and they expected to bargain then as Mexican shopkeepers do today. Most customers, too, felt satisfied only after haggling for their ware. In *A Book of New England,* Zephrine Humphrey defends the peddler:

> He ran all the risk; for he might injure or lose the things he took in exchange for his goods and could never be perfectly sure of 'realizing' on them. Perhaps, thus, his rascally reputation began in natural prudence.

An individual peddler seemed to have an unwritten franchise; consequently many traveled the same route each tour. Nathaniel Hawthorne spoke of this after having met a peddler traveling from Northampton to Worcester, Massachusetts, by stagecoach.

The pedlar was good-natured and communicative, and spoke very frankly about his trade, which he seemed to like better than farming. . . . He spoke of the trials of temper to which pedlars are subjected, but said that it was necessary to be forbearing, because the same road must be traveled again and again.

Donald Glasgow, a Massachusetts peddler, had a reputation for integrity that was unsurpassed. The little Scotsman took up his trade during the 1800s, after his doctor had diagnosed "consumption" and prescribed out-of-doors work. Customers grew to know that his steelyards were always accurate, his cart full of well-made ware. Donald kept at his trade for decades, declaring at last:

I wouldn't be happy away from the cart. The old horse has aye grown old, and so has Donald; my e'en are fair worn out, and the hills are steep to climb; but we are going on yet, please God, the cart and I.

Apprentices, Toolmakers, Decorators, and Peddlers in Connecticut

Connecticut is dotted now with antique shops, its cities are favorite spots for winter antique shows, its villages perfect sites for summer flea markets. Main highways are excellent and one can get from surrounding states to almost any point in Connecticut in half a day. The state is a Mecca for antiquers. Prices in many shops are high but the quality of the antiques is, in general, also high. In this area, where tremendous quantities of tinware were manufactured in the eighteenth and nineteenth centuries, some tinware can still be found.

THE APPRENTICE-SHIP SYSTEM

Massachusetts is remembered for Shem Drowne and the smiths who manufactured the first tin machines; Connecticut became prominent in the industry because of the number of apprentices its master smiths trained and because of its peddlers who were, according to one smith, "thick as toads after a rain."

THIS INDENTURE, made the *sixteenth* .... day of *April* - - - - in the year of our Lord one thousand eight hundred and *Eleven* - - - - **WITNESSETH, That** *Harry* - - - - - - - - son of *Jack Crane* - - - - *man* - - - - - - - - aged *Seventeen* - - - years *eight* - - - months, and *sixteen* - - - days, hath of his own free will and accord, by and with the consent of the said *Jack Crane* - - - - - - his *father* - - - - testified by his signature and seal to these presents, placed and bound himself an apprentice unto *Oliver Filley of Simsbury in the State* - - - of *Connecticut* - - - - - the county of Essex, and state of New-Jersey, to learn the art, trade, mystery, or occupation of a *Japaner of Tin ware* - - - - - - - - - - which the said *Oliver Filley* - - - - now useth, and with *him* the said *Oliver Filley* - - - - as an apprentice to dwell and serve for and during the term of *Three* - - - - - years, *three* - - - - - months, and *fourteen* - - - - days, from the date hereof, during all which term, the said apprentice his said master well and faithfully shall serve, his secrets keep, lawful commands do and obey; hurt to his said master he shall not do, nor wilfully suffer it to be done by others, but of the same, to the utmost of his power, shall forthwith give notice to his said master; the goods of his said master he shall not embezzle or waste, nor them lend, without his consent, to any; he shall not play at cards, dice, or any other unlawful game; he shall not frequent taverns or ale-houses; he shall not commit fornication nor contract matrimony; from the service of his said master he shall not, at any time, depart or absent himself without his said master's leave; but in all things, as a good and faithful apprentice, demean and behave himself towards his said master and all his, during the said term.— And the said master the said apprentice, the said trade, mystery, or occupation of a *Tin Japaner* - - shall and will teach, or cause to be taught well and sufficiently, in the best way and manner he can; and shall and will also find and allow unto the said apprentice *decent and sufficient wearing Apparel fitting for such an apprentice* - - - - - - - - - - -

and all other necessaries fit and convenient for such an apprentice, during the term aforesaid.

IN WITNESS WHEREOF, the parties to these presents, have hereunto interchangeably set their hands and seals, the day and year first above written.

Sealed and delivered in the presence of

Peter Freeman

David C. Bruce

Harry ✝ Crane
mark

Jack ✝ Crane
mark

Oliver Filley

Southampton, Conn.

Mr. Jedediah North

Sir:

I am informed that you are in want of an apprentice. I shall be glad to let you have my son and instruct him in your business according to your regulations. Please to give me an answer as soon as convenient. I can spare him as soon as you want.

Anson Matthews

America's first tinsmiths had been apprenticed to learn their trade in Europe. There they had been members of guilds, the forerunners of today's trade unions. When several European-trained tinmen settled in an American city, they formed a guild there, patterning their ways after familiar European customs. I have found no references to guilds in Boston, although there may well have been a sheet-metal-workers guild there, but such groups did exist in New York City, Philadelphia, Pennsylvania, and Albany, New York. In the latter city on August 8, 1788, a guild of tinmen and pewterers "with implements of their craft ornamented" marched in an "imposing procession" to celebrate New York State's ratification of the Federal Constitution.

In the apprenticeship system, still used in some of the trades, a master teaches his craft to young men who pay for their instruction with a given number of years of service. Early history books record colonial statutes which required that "all children not having estates otherwise to maintain themselves" were obliged to engage in a useful occupation, and apprenticeship was the usual way to learn such a "useful occupation."

Appenticeships varied in length from four to seven years. Earliest Massachusetts records refer most often to seven-year terms, although occasional four-, five-, and six-year terms are men-

Indenture. From Filley papers. Courtesy of Connecticut State Library, Hartford, Connecticut.

tioned. The clerk in a 1660 Boston Town meeting set down rules which were soon approximated throughout the colonies:

> Whereas itt is found by sad experience that youthes of this town, beinge put forth Apprentices to several manufactures and sciences but for three or four yeares time, contrary to the Customes of all well governed places, whence they are uncapable of becoming Artists in their trades besides their unmeetness at the expiration of their Apprenticeship to take charge of others for government and manuall instructions in their occupations which, if not timely amended, threatens the welfare of this town.
>
> Itt is therefore ordered that no person shall henceforth open a shop in this town, nor occupy any manufacture or science, till he hath completed 21 yeares of age nor except he hath served seven yeares apprenticeship by testimony under the hands of sufficient witnesses. And that all indentures made between master and servant be brought in and enrolled in the town's records written one month after the contract made or penalty of ten shillings to be payed by the master at the time of the Apprentices being made free.

A master was expected to act in a paternal manner toward his apprentices. Legally he was responsible for their actions as well as their wellbeing and their training, moral and professional. In 1665, the Duke of York decreed that children or apprentices who became "rude, stubborne or unruly," and who refused the counsel of their parents or masters were to suffer corporal punishment "not to exceed ten stripes" under the lash of the local law enforcement officer. There was an attempt, also, to protect young workers from harsh treatment; in 1644 a man and his wife were disciplined in Salem, Massachusetts Bay Colony:

> Hugh Laskm and his wife fined forty shillings for hard usuage of his late servant in victuals and clothes . . . the bed and clothing were not as should be. . . . One time the boy did not eat

until eleven o'clock. Goodman Balch said the boy was growing thin.

In 1642, one of the first compulsory education laws in America was enacted—a court order in the Massachusetts Bay Colony requiring masters to teach their apprentices to read and write. The Duke of York instituted a like law in the colony he governed in 1665. Night classes in reading and writing were held, and, by the eighteenth century, ciphering had become an additional requirement. Jonathan Stoughton of Windsor, Connecticut, was apprenticed to Nathan Day, blacksmith and whitesmith. The latter promised that Jonathan would learn the art of arithmetic to such proficiency that he might "keep a book well." A Connecticut order also commanded that "all masters of families do once a week at least catechise their children and servants [this included apprentices] in the grounds and principles of religion."

In the tinsmithing craft, a definite program was followed by an apprentice. From metal scraps he learned first to make cake stamps [now called cookie cutters], pill boxes, and calf weaners. Next he tried simple forms, such as basins, milk pans or pails, later tackling ware with more complicated shapes, requiring more pieces. A tin tazza or cake plate on a standard, a chandelier, or a crooked spout coffeepot required skill and practice.

Israel Horsfield, apprentice, wrote from one shop to another:

May the 29 1816

Mr. Oliver Filley
Windsor, Connecticut
To be left at the Hartford Post Office

Worthy Master, I take the liberty to write to you and let you know that I am in good spirits. I received a line from you this afternoon by Mr.

May the 29 1816

Worthy Master I take the liberty to Rite to you
and let you know that I am well and In good helth
I receeved a line from you this af ter noon by Mr
Brown and you In form med that you here
that I try to Doo too much In a day and don't
Doo my work well I must say my self that It
Has not ben So good as it oteo bee along back
But I in tend to doo my work better and have

I dare say that Mr filley made It as bad as it
was full She hee never found anny folt with my
Pails nor Dishkittels It was the pans that
he found the most folt with, It Is quite sick by now
here th people are taken verry sudden there has
several Died In this Lately, I like living here verry
Well In deed I have not Got acquainted much now
I don't want to nabd I have got acquainted with I
Leeke verry much, I shall I endeaver to doo as
well for you as I can and I shall ever respect
you as a frend for you was a frend to mee In time
of need and If you want mee to Goto the south
I wish that you would let me k no tha that I
Can calculate uppon Going and mr Hall says
If you want him to goo you must let him no
before his time Is out here Seiend my letter and I
wish that you would Give my best respects to
Mrs filley and all the family but almira
and her I don't care en athing about So I
am with respect your apprentist

To   Oliver   Israel Horsfield
     Filley

Brown and you informed that I try to do too much and dont do my work well. I must say myself that it was not so good as it otto bee back a long but I intend to do my work better and have. I daresay that Mr. Filley made it as bad as it was full, tho he never found any folt with my pails or my dish kittles. It was the pans he found most folt with. . . . I shall endeavor to do as well for you as I can and I shall ever respect you as a friend to me in my time of need. . . . So I end my letter and wish you to give my respects to all in the family except Almira, and her I don't care anything about. So I am with respect your apprenticest

Israel Horsfield

When an apprentice signed his name or his mark to an agreement, he made several pledges to abstain from many common pleasures. Rules such as these drawn up by one teetotaling master were not infrequent.

> The said Shaw is to be paid for the faithful performance of the above agreement 18 dollars and a pair of shoes, and if he does not get drunk above once in three months, a pair of stockings and his diet.

Principles agreed upon were sometimes ignored—by masters and by apprentices—and the pupils of one Deacon Nathan Elliot of Catskill, New York, were described as "a wild lot" who used to annoy him excessively by stealing and drinking his currant wine.

Adults of all ages have worried about their young folks, and after the Revolutionary War a gentleman commented:

> There was a great complaint of demoralization . . . that resulted from the war. Before the war nobody smoked, nobody used cards. Then apprentices and young folks kept the Sabbath and until sundown never left the house but to go to meeting. Now they go out more on the Sabbath than on any other day of the week. They say it is better than going to church to sit two hours and hear about hell.

Letter from apprentice Israel Horsfield to Oliver Filley. Courtesy of Connecticut State Library, Hartford, Connecticut.

Magazines such as *The Apprentices' Companion* appeared each month. These were designed to persuade all young people to follow habits of industry, temperance, and frugality.

When occasionally an apprentice deserted his master, the law discouraged benefactors, demanding a ten-shilling fine from anyone who harbored a runaway. One master smith wrote to his partner:

> You had better put off coming up. . . . I have a runaway apprentice here to work. I don't know if you have ever seen him but I think it likely you would know him.

EDWARD PATTISON, TINMAN

Although Shem Drowne was the first or one of the first to be a tinplate-worker in America, Edward Pattison probably influenced the growth of the industry more than Drowne or any other single smith: he introduced the manufacture of tinware in Connecticut, trained many apprentices there, and encouraged extensive tin peddling. (Many spellings of his surname are found, including Paterson and Patterson.) Edward was the oldest son of a large family living in Tyrone County, Ireland. In 1738, he shepherded two brothers and two sisters to America in order to fulfil a promise to his father. The Pattisons disembarked in Boston, then journeyed southwest to the vicinity of Berlin, Connecticut. There the young people found the countryside beautiful, its somewhat swampy soil fertile. Game was plentiful, and fish ran thick in the creeks branching off like veins from the Connecticut River. In spring a fisherman could fill a saddlebag or a bucket with shad or alewives in no time. Timothy Dwight, who in the early 1800s authored *Travels in New England and New York*, wrote:

> Berlin lies immediately north of Wallingford. Here the valley expands. . . . No township with-

in my knowledge which does not border on the ocean, a large or a small river, is equally beautiful with this. The soil is the richest kind; the groves thrifty; the vegetables luxuriant, and the interspersion of churches, houses, and fields delightful.

Edward, Anna, and William Pattison made their new home in this settlement which, in 1785, became the incorporated village of Berlin. (The other two Pattisons went farther south and have no further connection with the manufacture of tinware.) Anna became the mistress of a small house on Hart Street. It is not clear whether William was a tinsmith or a blacksmith, but there is no question about Edward, who went to work immediately, whittling wooden molds and making flat patterns for utensils of all sorts. When this was done he unpacked his wooden mallets and the sheets of tinplate brought down from Boston by team, and began shaping tinware.

As Pattison made tin pieces, curious neighbors nicknamed the Pattison workship Bang-All. After an assortment of utensils was finished, Edward polished the pieces with wood ashes and packed them in baskets to peddle. Decades later Emma Hart labored over this verse about a Berlin bride, Miss Tabitha Norton, and one of her wedding gifts:

> "Oh, what's that lordly gift so rare,
> That glitters forth in splendor's glare?
> Tell us, Miss Norton, is it silver?
> Is it from China, or Brazil, or —?"
> Thus all together on they ran;
> Quoth the good dame, "'Tis a Tin Pan,—
> The first made in the colony,
> The maker, Pattison's just by,
> From Ireland, in the last ship o'er.
> You all can buy. He'll soon make more!"

(The author of this verse became Emma Willard, remembered today as a feminist and forward-looking educator.)

A short time after Edward Pattison's first sales, leather-aproned apprentices were rubbing elbows in a new shop, and peddlers had to be hired to distribute their ware. By 1751, Edward felt prosperous enough to marry Elizabeth Hill, and they became the parents of several offspring: Lucretia, Lois, Edward, and Shubael. The boys followed their father's trade, and after his death in 1787 continued to supervise the flourishing business then called The Pattison Tinware Company. Their peddlers went farther afield than those of Edward, Sr.—south past Baltimore and north into Canada, where John Jacob Astor accompanied Shubael on trading trips.

For some years after the death of Edward, Sr., Berlin remained the hub of the tinware industry; more men and women were connected with the tinsmithing trade than with any other in the town. Some, like Hiram Mygatt, varnished the ware; or, like Polly Parsons, "flowered" it; others, like Elias Beckley and Jedediah North, made tinmen's tools.

That tin interests were overwhelming in Berlin's industry is reflected in this list of businesses made up soon after 1800:

 9 blacksmith shops
 9 wagon-building establishments
 2 clock factories
 2 broom factories
 4 cabinet shops
 6 tanneries
12 tin shops
 6 shops for making tinmen's tools
 1 shop for stamping tin- and copperware

FILLEY TINSMITHS

In the tinning trade the name of Filley became familiar in several states. Oliver Filley of Bloomfield (later Simsbury), Connecticut, was the first in the family to learn the trade. Born in 1784, Oliver was responsible for the family farm from the age of twelve, when his father died, until he began his new venture as a tinsmith soon after 1800. In 1805, he married Annis Humphrey who shared both his home and his business life until his death.

In 1810, Oliver was in Elizabeth, New Jersey, to set up a branch tin shop. Two decorators were there with him although he sent home asking Annis to have japanned ware sent on from Bloomfield. According to Oliver, "The inhabitants are making a great parade for Christmas here and tinware sells much better on that account." Apparently the New Jersey venture was a short-lived one, however, for soon Oliver was back in the home shop.

This Filley Bloomfield shop, like the Pattison one, was busy, and detailed ledgers passed down in the Filley family help to clarify our picture of this early industry. Tinsmiths, decorators, and peddlers made Oliver's shop their headquarters. Eldad Smith, William Root, Jared Lee, Oliver Brunson, Dan Wright, Ethan Judd, and Hiram Humphrey were among the tinsmiths. Oliver was kept active teaching his trade to relatives as well as to others. Among members of the family to enter the trade were Oliver's younger brother Harvey, his cousin Augustus, and his sons, Oliver Dwight, Jr., and Lucius. The master smith encouraged and advised members of the family who set up shops outside of Connecticut. He helped to finance, to order supplies, to train decorators; he shared his materials with the Filley tinsmiths who moved to Philadelphia, St. Louis, and Lansingburg, in New York (incorporated as part of the city of Troy in 1901).

MIGRATION OF TINMEN

The demand over the country for journeymen and master smiths eventually caused many to move from the tin centers where they had

Tinker Ted Marrott, piercing tin panels for a lantern. Courtesy of Old Sturbridge Village, Sturbridge, Massachusetts.

learned their trade to towns where there were no tinmen. Frequently they followed pioneer settlers South and West. It was a common practice for northern tinmen to take their tools to a town in the South agreed upon ahead of time with peddler acquaintances. Here the smiths worked for several weeks to furnish ware for northern peddlers traveling through southern states during winter and spring months. Northern roads at this time of year were unreliable and usually impassable. Augustus Kendall wrote: "One shop in Berlin employs sixty during the summer. In winter he moves to Philadelphia for the extension of his trade." In the fall of 1823, Bronson Alcott, doing a hitch as a tin peddler, along with fifteen other peddlers and tinmen, sailed from New Haven, Connecticut, to Norfolk, Virginia, aboard the sloop *Three Sisters*.

Manna Alderman of Burlington, Connecticut, was a peddler in the South for Elisha Dunham of Berlin, according to this contract:

> Burlington Sept 16th 1816
> Know all men by these presents that I, Elisha Dunham of Berlin, in Hartford County, State of Connecticut, do agree by these presents to pay Manna Alderman Twenty Five Dollars & one half the profits that shall arise on tin and other goods at the market price, per month. Said Alderman on his part is to peddle in North Carolina & its vissinity all kinds of artacles that is lawful to be sold & the said Alderman am to find own Horse & Wagon & Soforth.
>
> Elisha Dunham

Permanent settlement in new communities, of tinmen who had learned their trade in Connecticut, is illustrated by the Upson family. James Upson, who had been an apprentice of the Pattisons, opened a shop with his father-in-law, Joseph Cowles, in Marion, Connecticut, in 1790. Asahel and James, Jr., sons of the James who was the first Upson tinsmith, learned the trade and practiced it in Marion and in Cheshire until the mid-nineteenth century. James, Jr., had nine sons, one of whom—also named James—migrated to Mobile, Alabama, to set up shop. Four brothers followed him there. In 1849, this James, the third James Upson to be a tinsmith, followed the Gold Rush west to help fill the demand for tin basins used for panning. Meantime one of his brothers, who had mastered japanning along with tinsmithing, settled in Cincinnati to open a shop. These men had sons who were smiths and who, along with members of similar tinning families, spread their names and their trade from the East to the West Coast.

John Grannis, the first person to be granted a patent right to use the Parsons-Whiting tin machines in Cheshire, Connecticut, was also the first to request the right to use his machines in the southern states as well as at home. Eventually he paid one hundred dollars for the right to use the machines in Maryland, Delaware, Virginia, North and South Carolina, Georgia, and Ohio. A letter from Seth Peck, who with Asahel and David Peck had joined forces with the Dedham inventors in 1810, explains the arrangement with Grannis:

> Southington, Conn.
> 15th June 1810
>
> Mr. Calvin Whiting
> Dedham
>
> Sir
>
> The prospect brightens a little as Mr. John Grannis Tin Plate Worker of the town of Cheshire, County of New Haven and State of Connecticut is desirous to purchase our machinery and Patent Rights on the following terms—for his machine he pays cash on delivery, as respects the Patent Right he will pay one hundred dollars next Spring and wants liberty to use his Machines in the Southern States. At a certain season of the year, he will of course not use them in Cheshire so it amounts to using one sett of Machines. It is uncertain whether he will have occasion to use his Machines in the Southern States any considerable time – Mr. Grannis imagines that this will be the best plan we can adopt for disposing of the rights to those tinmen that wish to work in the Southern States as they often shift from place to place as they best accomodate their pedlars however they generally work all one winter in one place – Mr. Grannis is an intimate acquaintance of mine, and I think, should he purchase, will add to the interest in the Machinery – should these proposals meet your approbation you will please execute a deed as above or write us on the subject immediately.
>
> Yours to serve
> Seth Peck

P.S. The following statement will show the Rapid Progress of the Machines. Mr. Jared C. Lee yesterday under many disadvantages completed 60 lg. Pails – peaced bottoms – we venture to say were he to exert himself would come out but little short of 70 – Mr. Parsons of Berlin feels some inclination to purchase . . . nothing positive agreed on he merely talks favorable. Your letter of the 10th inst. my Father has received – the first object I conceive is to sell one or two rights which will then tend to agitate the minds of Tin-men.

S.P.

TIN MACHINES AND TOOLS IN CONNECTICUT

In 1810, Seth sailed for Columbia, South Carolina, to set up machines there after promising Whiting, "I intend to make some noise in South Carolina would I have the good fortune to arrive there in health."

The Pecks sold tin machines for years, and Seth was responsible for several improvements upon the original invention. Southington, Connecticut, became a center for the production of tin machines. Oliver Filley's papers include an agreement between Peck and himself allowing Filley and his heirs to "make, use and vend" the machine within the town of Windsor, Connecticut. This contract is dated 1818 and the rights were sold for twenty dollars. To my knowledge Oliver never did make machines although he did use and sell them. General use of the machines increased as they were improved; eventually they were capable of cutting, forming, braking, beading, slitting, cutting circles, stamping, and rolling metals. The 1835 advertisement of tinner Lyman Harrington from West Hartwick, New York, noted that he was using "Seth Peck's latest improved Patent Machines for manufacturing tin and copper ware."

In *Sketches of Southington*, Herman Timlow

lists tin-machine patents and inventions by Seth and other men who worked with him.

1819 – Seth Peck, machine for making tinware
1829 – Seth Peck, tinner's machine
1831 – Edward M. Converse, manufacturing ware from tin plate
1843 – Orrin and Noble Peck, machine for working sheet metal
1847 – Lester Smith, machine for manufacturing tin, copper, and other ware
1855 – Orson W. Stowe, machine for folding sheet metal
1858 – O. W. Stowe and Augustus Barnes, burring machine

Other inventors mentioned are Charles Raymond, Daniel Newton, and Enos Stowe. By 1870, the Southington machine company was called Peck, Stowe, and Wilcox. It employed five hundred men and paid the aggregate one thousand dollars a day.

Allen Buckley, a Berliner, made punches commonly used to cut circular pieces from tinplate. He is mentioned in communications between members of the Filley tinning family. In 1816, Augustus Filley of Lansingburg listed among his bills: "To pay Allen Buckley for a set of molasses cup punches—$5.00." In 1822 Oliver wrote to Henry James of New York City, mentioning James' order for blacking boxes, pill boxes, and canisters. The tinman boasted, "I have got a punch now and can make them handyer than when I first began." In 1830, Oliver Dwight Filley, Jr., who had set up shop in St. Louis, wrote to his father at home in Connecticut, the State of Blue Laws:

The large punch arrived two or three days back. . . . I find it much smaller than I ordered. I want it for pint cup bottoms, I want it not so heavy but it can be handled with one hand easy.

On December 19, 1831, O. D. Filley wrote again to his father asking him to arrange to have a set of tools sent west for a friend who was just starting in business. Individual tools and prices are listed:

1 hatchet swedge	4.00
1 large stake	13.00
1 creasing stake	3.50
1 blowhorn stake	3.75
1 square stake	2.50
1 candlemold stake	2.00
1 needlecase stake	2.00
1 set hollow punches	5.00
1 creasing swedge	5.00
1 collender swedge	4.50
1 large raising hammer	1.75
1 pr. shears	.50
1 double seaming stake	5.00
1 candlemold square stake	1.50
shears	1.00
1 set machines	125.00
1 large swedging machine the price of which will not be far from	25.00

In another note O. D. complained, "I bought a set of rollers for the small burring machine but Peck sent them without any cogs, a piece of carelessness in him which I want him to rectify." In 1832 O. D. sent from St. Louis for "a sett of first rate solid punches including the lantern punches. They may put up for my own use a die to make pill boxes like the ones in which Lees Pills are boxed with suitable hollow punches." Again, after receiving the punches, the smith wrote:

I have received Mr. Buckley's bill for the sett I ordered some time ago. I find that he makes but 4% discount on them and none at all on the extra tools which is a way of business to which I am not accustomed. On what principle they think I can afford to write, pay postage, talk and assist others to become competitors in business for nothing or next to it, I am at a loss to determine. And then to allow no discount on the extra tools, is what I call imposing on good nature. . . . I am well convinced that I can sell more tools than any agent they have, but they can not expect me to do a losing business to accomodate them.

JEDEDIAH NORTH AND HIS TOOL MANUFACTORY

O. D. bought from Jedediah North & Company of East Berlin, as well as from Buckley. The Connecticut Norths were metal-workers almost as soon as they were Americans. At first they were blacksmiths. Later members of the family worked in brass and in tin and were makers of scythes and pistols as well as tinsmiths' tools.

Jedediah North established a manufactory for tinners' tools in the late 1700s. He made chisels of all sorts, hammers, mallets, stakes, and punches, such as the prick punch used to make lanterns. His volume of business was large. A Maine tinsmith sent two pairs of shears with a peddler all the way to the Norths in Connecticut for repair. The North tool manufactory drew orders from points in all directions: from Jonathan Morrison in Portsmouth, New Hampshire; Nightingale McKim in Baltimore, Maryland; Lyman Gilbert, Harrisburg, Pennsylvania; Truman Cowles, Kingston, New York; William Werner, "Charleytown," South Carolina; Oliver Buckley, Stevens Plains, Maine.

Agents who sold tools for the Norths included Harvey Filley in Philadelphia, Pennsylvania; William Austin in Albany, New York; Augustus Filley in Lansingburg, New York; and Andrew Seger of New York City, who wrote:

Mr. Seth Peck has appointed me agent to sell Patent Machines for Working Tin. I think I shall have an opportunity to sell your tinsmiths' tools if you can allow me a reasonable commission.

Augustus Filley forwarded this letter:

Lansingburg,
March 24, 1823

Mr. North,

I inform you that I have not been able to leave home on account of roads . . . that is, before the snow left. Now it is so muddy that I do not think I shall be down until May. I may have a chance to send for the tools for David Cobble. They want you to have them sent on board the Lansing sloop direct to me. When they arrive I will take charge of them. . . . I shall be down in May. You can send more tools as soon as convenient and order them put on the Lansing sloop not to send them to Sheldon Newkirk as that you wrote me about.

Yours
Augustus Filley

If Jedediah could find him a journeyman, a Vermont smith wanted to place an order for tools.

1824

Bellows Falls, Vermont
Mr. Jedediah North

Sir:

Being at present in want of a journeyman at the tinware business I therefore forward to you this line to ascertain whether there is a young man of steady habits in your vicinity that I could employ for six months or a year. I wish you to make some inquiry and forward me a line would there be any, what his terms are, and if there is none I want an answer immediately that I may know where I can employ one. If you can find me one, I want to purchase of you a pair of shears and some other tools for my shop. If you succeed in procuring one and write me his terms I shall write you in return immediately on its coming. I wish for none but *a good workman*.

Respectifully yours,
Simon Pettis
(Written by James Thayer)

Another customer commended Jedediah, "I depend on your honesty that you will not charge me more as you sell them in general. Such a price I shall not dispute." Another, Burrage Yale, ordered tools and challenged, "My hope is that you will finish them in your best style, in other words, equal to Mr. Beckley's best manner." Several members of the North family worked in the factory. After Edmund, one of Jedediah's brothers was made a partner, the firm became the J. and E. North Company.

Oliver Buckley, a Connecticut man who had moved to Maine, did business with the Norths. (I have not been able to discover a relationship between Oliver and Allen Buckley, although it is probable that there was one.)

Dear Sir

Yours of Apr. 3 duly rec'd in good order. I rec'd a letter from Mr. Silas North at the same time he rec'd yours stating that he had sent a part and would send the remainder as soon as I should send you the money. . . . For now I must trubble you for one more sett of tools the same as I had before except two sett of . . . punches and one p. shears and the dubble seamer stake the big end 13 inches long. . . .

From yours respectably,
Oliver Buckley

In hast ples to excues errors.

TIN PEDDLING

Throughout the nineteenth century peddlers of all sorts gathered at political debates and at elections, on county-fair days and on militia days. A note from Canal Village, Massachusetts, mentions the presence on fair day of "a broom peddler, an indigo peddler, tin peddlers from Berlin, a clock peddler from Connecticut." Hundreds of young country fellows were hawking tinware, and many found both the adventure and the financial reward they sought. These Yankee salesmen roamed cow path and corduroy road up and down the Atlantic seaboard and inland. Timothy Dwight, preacher and traveler, commented, "I have seen them on Cape Cod and in the neighborhood of Lake Erie—distant from each other more then six hundred miles. They make their way to Detroit four hundred miles further—to Canada and to Kentucky, and if I mistake not, to New Orleans and St. Louis."

Tin peddlers were important economically, and popular socially, especially in rural areas. The English romantic poet, William Wordsworth, explained:

> By these itinerants, as experienced men,
> Counsel is given; contention they appease
> With gentle language; in remotest wilds
> Tears wipe away, and pleasant tidings bring;
> Could the proud quest of chivalry do more?

In 1849, Charlotte Wray Scott, who only a short while before had moved with her doctor-hus-

"Yankee Peddler" by John Whetten Ehninger (1827-1889). Courtesy of Newark Museum, Newark, New Jersey.

band from Granville, New York, to Garnaville,
Iowa, begged her brother Stephen Van Rens-
selaer Wray, a tin peddler, to make a trip to
Iowa.

> Rensselaer, where is he? Is he present at your
> family circle to hear this letter read? Is he able
> and stout enough to mount that high wagon and
> be off again, trying to earn something for another
> rainy day if such should come? If you would
> like to see me, Rens, you must come to Iowa.
> How I wish you would come. Do come, for I
> think you would make a fortune in a few months.
> There is but one store here and they are *so* high
> in their prices! Just think, fifty cts. for a fine
> tooth comb . . . it is scandalous. I have not seen
> a peddler since I have been here. It would be
> such a treat to see one. . . .

To an adult the visit of the peddler meant
gossip and news from distant places. Although
eventually "peddler's news" came to mean stale
news, farm folk were eager to hear the peddler
recall bits from the newspaper he had read two
weeks before, gossip related by a drover, an innkeeper or a toll-gate keeper, and messages sent
by friends along his route.

To a child the peddler personified romance.
He provided a tangible connection with that

vague world of people and towns beyond the horizon. Nineteenth-century boys dreamed of becoming peddlers as twentieth-century boys dream of exploring the moon. The usual peddler had a thrilling tale of adventure for each youngster he met; sometimes he parted with a souvenir —a shiny horn or an ABC plate. My father remembers Hiram LaHue, who always had a stick of peppermint candy or a chew of spruce gum for the young friends who held his horse or ran to get her a pail of water.

A peddler frequently mastered the jew's harp, the fiddle, or the ocarina, and many an evening was shortened by his playing, while the whole family sat around the hearth to sing. Frank Bresee was such a peddler-by-day, fiddler-by-night. When country folk heard that he was on the way, they planned a dance or a husking bee, and, for thirty-five cents, Frank fiddled away the night. Perhaps this was one of his calls:

Toy wooden peddler's cart and horses. Courtesy of The New-York Historical Society, New York City.

First couple leads to the right,
Swing four hands around.
Duck for the oyster, dive for the clam,
Look for the hole in the old tin pan.

Frank finally opened a store in Oneonta, New York, which grew into the Bresee Department Store owned by his descendants today.

Our first peddlers, those serious young Yankees in homespun breeches and jackets, with hand-knitted stockings dyed indigo blue or onion-skin yellow, walked from town to town. They sometimes used a "peddler's pony" or walking stick. Ware was packed ingeniously into baskets or tin trunks. Some peddlers pushed their goods in two-wheeled carts; others rode a single horse with a fifty-pound trunk swinging from each side of the saddle. Carts of varying sizes, drawn by one or more horses, became popular after 1800, when roads were somewhat improved.

It was an outfit such as this that came to be the trademark of the tin peddler. The construction of the cart was rather odd, with "wheels, axle-trees, arm and whiffle-trees like a light truck wagon, a large box for a body with an L in front to sit on. The body rested solid on the axle-tree, a rod was fitted to the off side to fasten to, and a rod some three feet long and sharp at the upper end was used to string sheepskins on." A peddler's cart resembled an old-time stagecoach with the top sawed off two thirds of the way down. It swung on straps—many broad ones laid one on top of the other, and fastened vertically upon the framework above the axles.

One gentleman reminisces that the cart seemed to him for all the world like the Trojan horse he had read about in school, and writer Della Lutes remembers that her mother always wanted kitchen cupboards with compartments exactly like those inside a tin cart. There were drawers under the seat for personal belongings—a cap, eggs, a jug of water or something livelier. The

Deed box. Notice strawberries. Collection of the author.

carts were always bright with paint—one in Connecticut was elegant in black and gold. Barney Koffman's from Wyoming County in western New York was bright green. Oftener they were red. Carter and Fiske outfits, which traveled over New England, boasted perfectly matched horses with silver-mounted harnesses. The tin carts were stores on wheels, decorated like the gaudiest of circus wagons.

The early peddler's lot was rarely an easy one. He was his own doctor, seldom without his asafoetida bag or his vial of turpentine to moisten his socks and ward off a cold. Frequently he was his own cook and his own mechanic—repairing damages to his vehicle or making do until he found a blacksmith shop. It was even difficult at times to find a decent place to sleep. Many peddlers camped out-of-doors, sleeping beside a brook or inside a haystack. At times innkeepers were known to place restrictions on their peddler guests, stipulating that no more than five could share one bed and that they must remove their boots before retiring.

Various working arrangements governed the peddlers. Some were hired by smiths. Such peddlers, who received a salary, took out a load of goods, sold it and returned, giving the smith the cash and the barter taken in. If the tinman knew the peddler well, he might send him out retaining only his IOU. When the salesman returned, he paid in cash or barter the wholesale price of the goods and kept what was left as his profit.

Odell Shepherd remarks in his biography of Bronson Alcott, one-time peddler:

> The War of 1812 had established even in the South a definite preference for American manufactures. The hills of New England were crowded with young men who could no longer

Large deed box. Courtesy of the late John Vrooman, Schenectady, New York.

find enough land to work. . . . In western Connecticut where the hills left the least arable land and also sent down the best mill-water, the development of a race of peddlers was as inevitable as the springing up of blueberries where fire has burnt the woods.

Hezekiah Griswold of Granby, Connecticut, vouched for his son and asked Oliver Filley's aid in 1824:

Capt. Oliver Filley

Sir –

My son the Bearor of this has a mind to try his luck in pedling – he informs me that as you was unacquainted with him your wish was to have a line from me. You, Sir, are alike unacquainted with me and my circumstances but should you be disposed to let him have any articles for pedling I hearby bind myself to see you paid – and, Sir, having this morning heard the state of your feelings and Character from Elder A. Balls, I take the liberty to entreat you to give my son all the instruction and information you think necessary and proper for him regarding the articles he should take and the manner in which he should proceed. He is young and unacquainted with business and much instruction and I shall count it a great favor to have you take the liberty to talk to him.

Contracts such as the following were often the basis for agreement between peddler and smith:

Know all men by these presents that I, Andrew Hays, of Granby, Connecticut, do agree to peddle tinware for Harvey Filley and Co. for the term of seven months (if the said Harvey wishes to have me so long.) If not the said Hays agrees to quit at any time said Filley wishes to have me and I am to allow said Filley one-half of what the license cost provided it can not be transferred over to another pedlar, I, the said Hays, agree not to waste, slander, or gamble away the said Filley's property but be industrious, prudent, faithful and true to my employers and I further agree that the said Filley shall not lose anything by me

Deed box with "Drape and Swag" border. Courtesy of James Stevens, Greenville, New York.

more than my wages and should there be any further loss, I will make it up to said Filley. I the said Hays, agree to furnish myself with a good horse, and wagon, harness, etc. and keep them in repair at my own expense, and for the same and my services I agree to take forty dollars a month.

And I, the said Filley & Co. agree to pay the said Hays at the expiration of same forty-five dollars a month provided the said Hays fills the contract as above stated.

Between 1775 and 1815, the tin industry stopped and started like a horse with the stringhalts; tinplate, still imported from Britain, was of course unobtainable during the Revolution and the War of 1812. By 1815, however, both foreign commerce and domestic industry had become more stable, and Berlin smiths alone made ten thousand boxes of tinplate into ware. Because so many sheets were cut up, finding a place to bury scraps was difficult. Berlin farmers for decades cursed as they dulled their plows on tin chips. Because so much metal lay beneath the street, a horse driven fast down Brandegee

DECORATED
WARE

Hill made a sound like chimes ringing. Tinmen's tools sold faster than hot cakes.

Shem Drowne's accounts mention only undecorated tinware. Before 1800, though, American-made gilt as well as japanned ware was advertised. John Burch, who had come to New York from London, advertised japanned ware in 1773, and we know from ledgers and correspondence that soon after 1800, Berlin smiths were hiring decorators to "flower." Similar decoration was practiced in New York, Pennsylvania, and in New England states other than Connecticut.

There were, throughout the nineteenth century, shops in the eastern states in which workers stenciled designs on tinware just as they stenciled patterns on Hitchcock-type chairs. Polly Parsons, who worked for the Filleys in 1811, was allowed $5.12½, or forty-one shillings, for two "gould patterns had of Mr. Lane." Probably these were stencils. At about the same time, Calvin Whiting was advertising "japanned and gilt tinware" in Dedham. (The term gilt was

(Left) Apple tray with white band typical of Connecticut. Courtesy of Old Sturbridge Village, Sturbridge, Massachusetts. (Right) Large canister with design typical of that associated with the Filleys. Courtesy of Anne Avery, Batavia, New York.

An Agreement and Bargain between Oliver Filley, of Simsbury, on the one part, and Joseph Brown Junr: of Windsor on the other, Hartford County, State of Connecticut ss:

1st On the part of Sd — Filley —

I the aforesaid Oliver Filley — do hereby agree and promise to employ the Sd Joseph Brown Junr. the term of twelve months from the 1st day of January 1811, at the business of Japaning, flowering and painting Tin Ware, in the Town of Simsbury aforesaid. and to teach him or cause him to be taught the Art, Trade or Mystery of Japaning, and making preparing and using all and every kind of Japan Varnish &c, and of making and preparing all kind of paints used in painting and flowering Tin Ware. so far as my knowledge does or may extend within the sd term of twelve months. Also to instruct him in the Art of painting and flowering such part of the time, within the Sd twelve Months as shall not necessarily be required in performing the business of Japaning &c, as aforesaid. And as a pecuniary compensation for his services; at the expiration of sd time, to pay unto him the sd Joseph Brown Junr. the Sum of Eighty Dollars, in Money; & to furnish him with board and Lodging

Secondly, On the part of Sd Brown.

I Joseph Brown Junr. aforesaid, do hereby agree and promise to serve the sd Oliver Filley, during the term, at the business, at the place and upon the considerations above named. according to my best faculties, with faithfulness & integrity, and divulge nothing relating the Arts or Mysteries aforesaid, to any person. whereby the Sd Filley may receive injury.

Augustus Filley
Jacob Williams

Simsbury Feb. 18th 1811.

Joseph Brown Junr.
Oliver Filley

used to mean decoration with gold leaf.) Bronzing identifies stenciling with bronze powders. Usually "decoration" in this volume refers to the freehand ornamentation in oils known to many as country painting.

Often an apprentice learned both the arts of japanning and flowering, and women as well as men frequently learned these particular skills. A contract between Oliver Filley and Joseph Brown, Jr., of Windsor, was quite specific:

An agreement and bargain between Oliver Filley of Simsbury, on the one part, and Joseph Brown, Jun. of Windsor on the other, Hartford County, State of Connecticut:

On the part of said Filley:

I, the aforesaid Filley, do hereby agree and promise to employ the sd. Brown the term of twelve months from the first day of January 1811, at the business of japanning, flowering and painting Tinware in the town of Simsbury aforesaid and to teach him or cause him to be taught the Art, Trade and Mystery of Japanning, and making and preparing all kinds of paints used in painting and flowering Tin Ware, so far as my knowledge does or may extend during the said term of twelve months. Also to instruct him in the Art of Painting and Flowering Tin Ware such part of the time within the said twelve months as shall not necessarily be required in performing the business of japanning, etc. aforesaid. And as a pecuniary compensation for his services, at the expiration of said time, to pay unto him, the Sd. Brown, the sum of Eighty Dollars, in Money, and to furnish him with board.

Secondly: On the part of Sd. Brown:

I, Joseph Brown, Jun. aforesaid, do hereby agree, and promise, to serve the Sd. Filley, during the term, at the business, at the place, and upon the consideration above named, according to my best facilities, with faithfulness and integrity, and divulge nothing relating to the Arts or Mysteries aforesaid, to any person, whereby the Sd. Oliver Filley may receive injury.

Employment agreement between Oliver Filley and Joseph Brown, Jr. Courtesy of Connecticut State Library, Hartford, Connecticut.

Windsor 22 April 1824

Mr. H. Tilley Your letter of the 11th April has been
read it informed me that you wanted the two girls
but not their father the workeman, I last satturday went
again to Berlin but could not make the bargain
with the girls one of them I suppose by what I could
find out is a going to get married the other is Young
and would not go out allone and her father wanted
her to go out to Rochester with him he had wrote a letter
to Mr. Hubbard Rochester stating what he & his girl the painter
would go out for before Stiel saw him and had put
into the post office but I made him go and take it
back — untill I could here from you but some of Hubb.
friends found it out and they made him put it into the
office again so the stands that If Hubbard will give
him what he askes, for his girl he will have to go —
I then came a cross a Mrs. Bennett who it is sayd
is a good painter she has been to Baltimore two or
three Seasons I agred to give her two Dollars a week
for a year & bare her expences on & Back — I have
given her ten Dollars in cash to bare her expences
on and charged the same to you she has agred to go
as soon as they possibly can, or as soon as Esqr
Dunham will sellrase her which he thinks will take
fore or 5 weeks but he will let her come as
soon as he can, I know you are in an imediate
want but I could not do any better If you think best
it may so happen that I can hire this Young Hulbert girl
by giving her 13/6 a week provided she does not go to rochester
her Mother had rather she would go to Philadelphia than to Rochester
but would not agree as she should then, you will write & direct about
it, there is a Miss Abigal Williams who understands Japanning &
wishes to learn to Paint She will work for you one year for
a Dollar & a quarter a week and give in five weeks time to
learn to Paint in If you want her write I cannot get
any Boy for you she I expect would learn to paint handy
and would like to paint the greatest part of the time. there
has been a great call for painters in this Quarter and they
are Very Scarce and Young —   Oliver Tilley &

Women to flower tinware were at a premium in Berlin at least from 1810 until 1820. The Miss Parsons mentioned previously was given a dollar bonus to start work in the Simsbury Filley shop, although apparently she had worked for Oliver in Elizabeth the season before. Sarah Manning Upson, second wife of Salmon Upson, ornamented ware from his family's shop. There were probably women painters in every tin family. Despite this, Oliver Filley, in a letter written in 1824 to his brother Harvey, explains some of the difficulties in hiring competent decorators.

Mr. H. Filley

Your letter of the 11th April has been rec'd. It informed me that you wanted the two girls but not their father the workman. I last Saturday went to Berlin but could not make the bargain with the girls. One of them I suppose from what I can find out is going to get married. The other is young and would not go on all alone and her father wanted her to go to Rochester with him. He had wrote a letter to Mr. Hubbard, Rochester, stating that he and his girl, the painter, would go out, before I had first saw him and had put it in the post office but I made him take it out – Until I could hear from you but some of Hubbard's friends found it out and they made him put it in the post office again so the case stands that if Hubbard will give him what he asks for himself and his girl he will have to go. I then came across a Mrs. Bennett who it is said is a good painter and has been to Baltimore two or three seasons. I agreed to give her two dollars a week for a year and bare her expenses on and charge the same to you. She has agreed to go as soon as Esq. Dunham will release her which he thinks will take fore or five weeks but he will let her come as soon as she can, I know you are in immediate want but I could not do any better. If you think best it may happen that I can hire this Hulbert girl by giving her ten shillings, eight pence a week provided she does not go to Rochester. Her mother would rather she would go to Philadelphia than to Rochester

Letter concerning decorators from Oliver Filley to Harvey Filley. Courtesy of Connecticut State Library, Hartford, Connecticut.

but would not agree as she should then. You will write to direct about it. There is a Miss Abigail Williams who understands japanning and wishes to learn to paint. She will work for you for a dollar and a quarter a week and give in six weeks' time to learn to paint if you want her. I can not get any Boy for you, she, I expect, would learn to paint handy and would want to paint the greatest part of the time. There has been a great call for painters in these quarters and they are verry scarce.

Yours
Oliver Filley

Hiram Mygatt, an ornamental coach painter in Berlin, had a shop at the back of his premises where tin was japanned and baked. Mr. Dunham, tinsmith, also had a decorating shop in Bloomfield in the 1820s. Edward Francis was a japanner

Document box with unusual bold design in yellow. Courtesy of Bernice Drury, Springfield, Vermont.

(Left) Deed box with expert brush stroking. Red has orange tint. Courtesy of Frances Elliot, Saugerties, New York. (Right) Oval box with peculiar orangy blossoms and fine details in black. Courtesy of Old Sturbridge Village, Sturbridge, Massachusetts.

who worked for years in the Filley shops: for Oliver in Connecticut, for Harvey in Philadelphia, and for Augustus in Lansingburg, New York. Obviously japanners as well as painters moved from shop to shop, from town to town, from master to master. Oliver wrote to Harvey: "Edward Francis is here now making varnish for me. I will get him to work awhile and ship you on some Japan Tin such as I have." Again, "Francis says he will go on for you for a year at the same rate as he did before only he will not agree to work only when he is able but will pay for his board when he lyes still."

Decoration from Connecticut is difficult to identify as such except through a study of pieces found in that state. Few pieces signed by known decorators there have been identified. I am familiar with a coffeepot which is marked "William Eno, Simsbury, Conn.," but I have not been able to find whether this man was decorator, peddler, or owner of the coffeepot. Documents at the Connecticut State Library suggest that he was born in 1795 or 1796 and that he died in 1838. Another piece is marked "This box was made by Hallam Whiting 1810-1830 Stonington, Conn." The box is painted, but, of course, no one knows whether or not Mr. Whiting dec-

Deed box with rare acorn pattern. Yellow on acorn "cup" is fingertip blended. Courtesy of Cooper Union Museum, New York City.

orated it. Shirley Spaulding Devoe identifies the work of Sarah Upson with a picture and article in the July, 1961, *The Connecticut Historical Society Bulletin*.

Fortunately, a few pieces of tinware have been cherished by descendants of the Filley tinmen, and other pieces with similar designs have been found along the routes followed by their peddlers. Decorated as well as plain ware was sold from the Connecticut, Philadelphia, and York State shops, although correspondence from O. D. in St. Louis makes no reference to painted ware. Occasionally finished pieces were shipped from shop to shop; in 1818, Augustus asked Oliver for "24 rimmed waiters, some with birds on them, if you please." (I have seen a coffeepot ornamented with a bird resembling a goldfinch—the wings are dark green; this pot has the date 1819 scratched in the japan on the bottom.)

I suspect that the wives of Oliver and Augustus were painters. When Oliver was in New Jersey he wrote to Annis, "I wish you to do everything in your power to get a large quantity of japanned tin on hand and have it well done and a good assortment for I expect to send on a panel here, for we can not, with what help we have, do it as fast as we want to sell it." And, for some reason, perhaps because she was a decorator, Amelia Filley was on the payroll of her husband, Augustus. An item for March 6, 1816, reads "Due Amelia Filley — $80.50." Between September, 1816, and February, 1818, I found payments to Amelia of $174.

There are two general types of decoration that I believe are typical of Filley painting. In one type a white band or circle is used and the japanned background is usually thin and lustrous, not the black indigenous to Maine and used by the Butlers of New York State. The decoration has a repeat border using a bright vermilion with alizarin crimson and white overstrokes, a bright green—more blue than yellow

Large deed box. Courtesy of James Stevens, Greenville, New York.

Bread tray in red with
pattern thought to be
typically Filley. All yellow
designs on ends. Courtesy of
the Philadelphia Museum of
Art, Philadelphia,
Pennsylvania.

—and yellow ochre. There is often a combination of fruit and flowers with green leaves and
black tendrils. Such borders are found on bread
trays, octagonal trays, caddies, and deed boxes.
They are done freely and expertly, and designs
are well balanced in form and color. Sometimes
the borders are used in conjunction with a
larger design, perhaps a spray of flowers and
leaves of the same colors used in the border. A
second type of design that seems to be a Filley
pattern (if one can designate any designs in such
a way since decorators moved from shop to
shop) is also on a white band or circle. These
patterns have one difference in color and another in technique; the red used is orangy, and
the colors are blended by using a fingertip to
apply yellow on the orange-vermilion, or yellow
on blue, or white on red or blue or vice versa.
Peaches, pears, acorns and shells have been used
in repeat borders, with fine black tendrils and
veins and details on flowers and fruit. Sometimes these motifs are rearranged to fit a white
circle on a coffeepot or a deed box. The yellow

brush strokes used in secondary borders are abundant and carefully executed. In all probability many types of ornamentation flowed from Filley shops since these operated over a long span of years in different localities. Eventually probably local artists in Philadelphia and Lansingburg were taught to flower and to incorporate their ideas in designs that were different.

The Stevenses of Stevens Plains, Maine; Other Maine Smiths and Peddlers

DISTINCTIVE SHAPES and colors give character to the tinware native to Maine. Old tin trunks are frequently flat rather than domed. Coffeepot spouts sometimes curve downward at the tip and are neither hooked nor straight like those from other areas. Yellow and white as background colors are used more frequently than anywhere else and red is found occasionally. Maine tinware was distributed widely by peddlers so that it is found today in Canada, New Hampshire, and Massachusetts as well as in Maine. This whole northeast section is a thrilling one for the collector of tinware because he can identify at first glance some of the tinware he finds here.

A FAMILY
TRADE

The family was an important unit in the tinsmithing, decorating, and peddling trades, and life within different tinning families showed little variation, with men apprenticed to learn their trade and mothers teaching daughters to "flower" or "japan." Often only locale and names were different. Many of the tinmen were acquainted with each other; they learned together and worked together; they intermarried; they borrowed tinplate from each other and acted as each other's agents.

In Maine during the early 1800s, local folk were amused by a dance of the Penobscot Indians. It was called Pe'dles be'djose—"The peddler is coming." The Indians chanted:

> The peddler is coming, ya-hi-ho,
> He has money, ya-hi-ho,

and made pantomimes mimicking a peddler overloaded with bulky ware. This comical pastime was undoubtedly inspired by the group of men and women who lived at Stevens Plains, a community about three miles west of Portland. The Plains stretch for a mile or more across a sandy expanse dotted with maple and elm trees. (Over the years this village has also been called Westbrook and Deering.)

THE STEVENS FAMILY AND OTHER MAINE TINMEN

The original town was named after the family of Isaac Sawyer Stevens, a blacksmith who owned a two-story frame building erected in 1767, the first home in this locality. During the Revolutionary War, while Isaac was soldiering, his wife Sarah turned the house into an inn. Meantime other folks came to settle and, as was the custom, they built their homes near the inn.

Zachariah Brackett Stevens, Isaac and Sarah's fourth child, was born in 1778. When he learned the tinsmithing trade—I have been unable to find *where* he learned it—he set a pattern which many young Maine men were to follow. Stevens Plains, like Dedham, Massachusetts, and Berlin, Connecticut, became a tin center.

Zachariah opened a shop in 1798 where he made and decorated all kinds of tinware. He taught others his trade and sent out ware on peddlers' wagons. According to Esther Stevens Brazer, Zachariah, who was her great-great-grandfather, was a deeply religious man "positive in his convictions" like many of New England's descendants from the Puritans. With Zachariah it was "either friend or enemy, but far more friends than enemies."

Miriam was the tinsmith's wife, and the couple had two sons, Alfred and Samuel, who became tinsmiths, and two daughters, Emmaline and Cordelia. Some of Zachariah's finest painting has been found on pieces he made for members of his family: an octagonal pincushion box for Emmaline, a pair of monogrammed flower-holders for Miriam, a large box which Alfred used when he was surveying.

Uncle Zach, as he was known in his community, established a store beside his tinshop and interested himself in politics. In 1823 he was coroner; at later dates he was selectman, deputy sheriff, and postmaster.

In about 1830, Zachariah turned his shop over to his sons. In 1832 the Stevens shop was one of eleven tinshops on the Plains, which during that year manufactured ware worth twenty-seven thousand, three hundred dollars. The peddling of goods and the acquiring of barter constituted an important part of the business. The long, wooden shed behind the tinshop where barter was dumped, sorted, and stored temporarily, stood until about 1900 when it was destroyed along with the last of the tin carts which had been kept there.

A report in the *Argus* tells of the destruction of the Stevens shops in 1842:

> Fire broke out this morning about two o'clock at Stevens Plains, in the blacksmith shop of Z. B. Stevens and soon communicated to the [tin] shop of his son Samuel B. Stevens. Both shops were

consumed. Mr. S. B. Stevens lost his books, ware, tin plate, etc., amounting to $1500. Insured $300. . . . The citizens turned out with great spirit, and disputed ground with the fire adversary so successfully that the buildings nearby contiguous to those destroyed were saved, including a large amount of property.

Although the best known, the Stevenses were not the only early tinsmiths on the Plains. Thomas Briscoe arrived in 1803. He was said to have served his apprenticeship in Britain, then to have migrated to Boston where he married Sarah Rose, niece of Paul Revere. An old-timer of the area, reminiscing in 1888 in the Portland *Argus* about Briscoe, commented: "We think that Mr. Briscoe might have been the first tinman, pedlar, and tinker. Who was the *first pedlar* in Maine? We think Old Briscoe was that man." A second note is found in a later newspaper:

In the *Argus* of April 10 was a very entertaining letter, at least to one resident of the Plains, an old man now, weighted tremblingly down with the burden of more than four score years. It was a familiar reminiscence to have so forcibly brought to mind the names of familiar friends and companions, bearing the business cognomen of "tin-plate-workers." Uncle Briscoe

(Left to right) Oval box. Courtesy of Marian Poor, Augusta, Maine. Tall caddy. Courtesy of Gina Martin, Wapping, Connecticut. Flat-topped deed box. Courtesy of Bernice Drury, Springfield, Vermont. Decoration on three pieces appears to be that of Stevens Plains painters. Photograph from The Historical Society of Early American Decoration.

passed in retrospection before me, and his novel
conveyance, which was like the dump trucks of
today, having but two wheels, whereby his horse
could feed along the roadside, waiting patiently
his master's pleasure.

The Briscoes adopted five daughters, the children of Sarah's sister, Mary Francis. Perhaps all
of these women drove Thomas to drink, for old
records say that he never was a financial success
because of his overfondness for "twitcheye."

Soberer smiths found their way to the Plains.
Elisha and Elijah North and Oliver Buckley arrived from Connecticut to set up shops and teach
apprentices. Soon they, too, were sending out
ware by peddlers. In the first decades of the nineteenth century, journeymen apprentices and
peddlers swarmed out from the Plains to Bangor,
along the coast, and to towns bordering the
Penobscot and Kennebec rivers.

Tinmen applauded the arrival of Isaiah, Ebenezer, and Chauncey Woodford, who also migrated from Connecticut to the Plains; these men
were comb-makers, and horn combs were among
the most popular of the sundries sold from many
tin carts. (The Woodfords manufactured more
than enough combs to supply Maine peddlers,
and they sold in large quantities to buyers in
Boston, New York City, and Philadelphia.)

Pewter ware, first cousin to the ware made
from tinplate, was also produced in quantities in
Stevens Plains. The brothers Freeman and Allen
Porter were pewterers there. And Frederick
Dunham describes the first visit his father Rufus,
another pewterer, made to the Plains:

> On Sunday with a companion he strolled in
> the country to Stevens Plains, West Brook, three
> miles from Portland. At that time the place was
> very much alive since it was the headquarters
> for a hundred or more pedlars whose markets

4.

Do not sell any Barter without permission

LIST OF BARTER BOUGHT BY MORILLO NOYES,

BURLINGTON, VT. *Nov. 25th* 1854.

PRICES SUBJECT TO THE FLUCTUATIONS OF THE MARKETS FROM TIME TO TIME.

Item			@		Item			@	
Sheep Pelts,		12	@	50	Flint cut glass,	per lb.	2	@	
Wool, Fleece, washed,	per lb.	25		35	Eggs, fresh,	per doz.	17		
do do unwashed,	"	17	—	25	Horns, average lots,	each.	1		1½
do do Black and Cotted,	"	17	—	25	do ox,	"	3		5
do Pulled, washed,	"	20	—	28	Mustard seed,	per qt	8		
do do unwashed,	"	18	—	25	Old Silver, good,	per oz.	100		
do Tag, free from manure,	"	8	—	15	do Gold, Jeweler's,	per pwt	25	—	37½
do Coarse and broken do	"	8	—	15	do do good,	"	37½	—	50
Feathers, Geese, new and good,	"	50			Socks, all wool,	per pair.	not wanted		
do Hens, do	"	8			do part cotton,	"			
do Turkies, do	"	4			do all cotton,	"			
Copper, free from iron and dirt,	"	15			Stockings, woolen,	"			
Brass, do do do	"	12			Mittens, do plain,	"			
Pewter, do do do	"	15			do do fringed,	"			
Lead, Tea,	"	3			Flannel 4-4 all wool,	per yard.			
do Solid,	"	3			do 4-4 part cotton,	"			
Rags, white and clean,	"	6			Tow cloth 4-4, all linen,	"	15	—	20
do Brown, free of woolens and papers,	"	3			do do 4-4, part linen,	"	12	—	17
do mixed, do do do do	"	3¼	—	4	Strainer cloth, all linen,	"	20	—	25
do soft woolen,	"	2			do do part linen,	"	15	—	25
do News papers,	"	½			Fox, Black and silver,				
Bristles, good and well combed,	"	6	—	25	do Red, prime,		75	—	87½
do do and uncombed,	"	2	—	10	do do unprime,		6	—	62½
Apples, dry, light and tart,	"	5			do cross prime,		100	—	2.00
Strawberries, dry, nice and good,	"	12			do do unprime,		25	—	1.00
Raspberries, do do do	"	12			Fisher, prime and large,		100	—	2.50
Blackberries, do do do	"	12			do unprime,		75	—	1.50
Currants, do do do	"	8			Lynx, prime.				
Butter, store and common,	"	12		16	do unprime,				
do good dairy,	"	17	—	20	Bear, prime and large,		3.00	—	6.00
Lard, good,	"	11	—	12½	do unprime, cubs,		1.00	—	3.00
Sugar, Maple, good caked,	"	6		8	Otter,				
do do dry tubbed and good,	"	6	—	7	Beaver,				
Hair, long, 18 inches and over,	"	20			Raccoon, good colors and prime,		10	—	25
do short cattle tails, &c.	"	6			do poor and unprime,		0	—	10
do women's, good colors	"	17	—	25	Minks, prime and large,		100	—	1.25
do " poor do	"	5	—	10	do poor and unprime,		6	—	50
Deer skins, Red coats,	"	20	—	25	House cat, prime and good,		4	—	8
do do Blue do	"	20	—	23	do poor and kittens,		2	—	4
do do Gray do	"	10	—	15	Musk Rats, prime,		3	—	5
Beeswax, free from grease,	"	25			do poor and kittens,		0	—	1½
Cattle Sizing, good pates, ears and skirts,	"	2	—	2½	Marten or Sable, prime,		100		
do do Beamings and Skeivings,	"	1	—	1½	do do unprime,		25	—	50
Good Flax, well dressed,	"	8	—	10	Dairy Skins,		12	—	42
Old Rubber, pure,	"	17	—	25	Calf Skins,	per lb.			
Woolen yarn,	"	42	—	50	Dry Sheeps skins,	each.	0		6

Weasels, Woodchucks, & Squirrels, worthless,   *Old Wro't & Cast Iron 1 ct. pr.*

were in Northern New England, Canada and along the coast of Maine, New Brunswick and Nova Scotia. The windows of the different factories where were made high backed combs, brooms, tinware, decorated japan ware, brushes and pewter ware so fascinated him that, in the following week, he asked for time off so that he might see the works in operation.

Soon after this visit Rufus settled in Stevens Plains where he made and peddled pewter ware. Winters were severe and most roads impassable. One road to Montreal via Crawford Notch, New Hampshire, Lydonville and Derby Line, Vermont, and Coaticook, Quebec, however, remained open, the snow packed down by traffic. Four- and six-horse vans carried freight from Canada to Portland for shipment by boat to Boston. Dunham loaded a wagon each winter with his ware and drove north to barter for furs, hides, sheep pelts, yarn, stockings, mittens, ox tails, hog bristles, and cattle horns. According to Frederick, Rufus found it easy to send his hides and pelts back home: teamsters welcomed them to spread over the loads they were carting to the coast.

BARTERING

Customers were pleased by the peddler's acceptance of barter rather than hard cash, scarce as hens' teeth throughout the nineteenth century —especially in rural sections. Every farm wife could find something she was about to discard which the peddler would take in exchange for a piece or two of tinware. Will, who does not identify himself further, explains in an April, 1888, letter to the editor of the Portland *Argus*:

List of barter accepted by peddlers working for master tinsmith Morillo Noyes. Courtesy of Baker Library, Harvard University, Cambridge, Massachusetts.

> Soon the horses and man returned, drawing the cart under a load of truck as large as a load of hay, consisting of paper rags, wool, wool slats, [sheepskins with the wool off] hogs' bristles, old copper, brass and block tin, and all sorts of pel-

fry, etc., generally worth double what they started off with. Paper rags were then worth four to ten cents a pound. . . . Those who traded with the pedlar in those days paid him no money, but let him have at his price such as they did not know what to do with. The horse and carts, the "tin team" improved from year to year. . . . His [the peddler's] unique method of trading, too, would stagger some of the avaricious tradesmen of today. Money was not plentiful and when he found he could not make a bargain he would banter them for their old dippers, receiving with them a few pennies in exchange for new, go on his way rejoicing, presumably repairing some of them for future use, while others would be tossed to the wayside as rubbish, leaving his patrons delighted in the possession of a new drinking cup.

An elderly acquaintance of mine remembers that to his surprise, no matter how much barter his mother had saved, at each visit her peddler allowed her exactly six cents toward a new purchase.

Some peddlers carried carefully whittled clothespins to use as small change, so that they, too, might keep their hard money.

Actually, little hard money circulated, and each area discounted paper money at a different rate. No wonder barter continued during this confusion. By 1850, the list of items acceptable by tin peddlers as barter was long—including everything from caraway seeds to kitten skins. The list that Morillo Noyes, a Burlington, Vermont, master smith posted for his peddlers included feathers, lard, preserved or dried fruit, maple sugar, beeswax, flint glass, old silver and gold, woven cloth. The barter trade alone netted Noyes from eight to ten thousand dollars a year.

Many of the tin manufactories had large warehouses where barter was sorted and baled, like

Teapot with kind of decoration attributed to Oliver Buckley of Stevens Plains, Maine. Courtesy of Mrs. J. B. Watts, Old Tappan, New Jersey.

that of the Tracy Brothers in Ballston Spa, New York. Their rag room was 40 by 80 feet, and eight or ten women worked there at a time, sorting rags into a half dozen or so grades. The building was three stories high and sorting started on the top floor. Rags were sent down chutes to baling rooms. Massachusetts paper mills constantly needed rags of different qualities and paid well for them. Hides were sent to leather factories to be tanned; wool from sheepskins was carted away to be woven into fabrics such as those called "butternut" and "frocking." Horns and hoofs made glue, sizing, and combs. Brush-makers purchased bristles. Metal junk went to Boston—even tin chips—worth one cent a pound delivered at the wharf. Wood ashes went to the potasheries for fertilizer or to the soap factories. Fur pelts were sold to hatters like Mr. Booth of Berlin, a gentleman with an ear trumpet who always claimed to hear exactly half the price demanded by those who took him beaver pelts.

Sometimes tinmen, themselves, were interested in industries which made use of their barter.

Maine coffeepot with rare painted cornucopia, curved spout. Courtesy of Mrs. Burleigh, Wiscasset, Maine.

Shubael Pattison and Benjamin Wilcox of Berlin, Connecticut, were partners in the manufacture of textiles. Pattison also had a shop where girls made muffs from furs brought down from Canada. So the tin peddler, indirectly, helped to build infant industries that were breaking out over the country like a rash during the late eighteenth and the nineteenth centuries.

(It is interesting to discover that tinware, itself, became an item to be bartered. It was used especially in trading with the Indians for furs. An exchange list at a trading-post near the Niagara River announced that one gallon-size tin kettle would be exchanged for the hides of two bucks. Small mirrors with tin frames were used for Indian trade, too.)

A FEW PECULIAR PEDDLERS

There are stories of peddlers over the country who became legends because they were odd. Cling Clang deserves Maine's "Most Peculiar

Peddler" award. Downeasterners, relaxing after a day of hunting or fishing, still tell stories about this peddler who jumped from Maine to Nova Scotia and back with a bag of tinware over his shoulder and a brass-tipped pole in each hand. His nickname came, of course, from the noise he made as he vaulted along—they say he could be heard a half mile away as he flew eight or ten feet with each leap, swinging easily over brooks and fences.

No one remembers this peddler in store clothes; he contrived his garments from gunny sacks and went barefoot each year until the ground froze. Tangled locks streamed behind him as he traveled, for he never wore a cap or visited a barber. Cling Clang's habits were as strange as his appearance. A barrelhead was a permanent part of his paraphernalia; in the daytime this was his seat and at night it cradled his head. Those who knew him best also noted his unusual eating habits. Cling Clang never mixed his foods: he would drink tea clear, then eat a

Yellow Maine box with cherry motif thought to be typical of the painting of Zachariah Stevens. Collection of the author.

spoonful of sugar. But the thing that Maine folk remember best about him is his dread of roosters. Mischievous boys of Swan's Island, knowing his aversion, freed a pet rooster near him as he slept. When the rooster crowed, the peddler rushed from the shed where he had stayed over night to vault off crying as if he were in anguish.

Cling Clang rarely lingered indoors, even to sleep. One winter's day his friends in Sullivan, Maine, found him under a boat, frozen, clutching the barrelhead which had worn as thin and fragile as the old peddler himself.

Milo Wells, a conniving peddler who toured New England, was a veteran of the Civil War. (In some states there were laws prohibiting the able-bodied from the occupation of peddling. Consequently after the war there were many peddlers who had been handicapped by battle or by accident.) On one nippy, frost-filled evening Milo craved a warm and comfortable bed. After having been refused several times, since he had gained a certain notoriety because of his fondness for hard cider and New England rum, he hit upon a scheme. Despite the late hour, Milo headed for a darkened farmhouse where he hammered briskly on the door. When a sleepy voice from the window above asked what he wanted, Milo inquired whether or not the farmer would like to buy some tinware.

"Why in tunket are ye a-tryin' t' peddle tinware in the middle of the night?" asked the man.

The peddler explained that he had not been able to find a place to sleep and had decided to work all night. As Milo anticipated, the farmer ordered him to put his horse in the barn and come on in to bed.

Three other post-Civil War peddlers, although they lived outside of Maine, were handicapped

Maine ware. Small flat-topped box typical of that state. Coffin-lid tray is large, pieced. Courtesy of The Historical Society of Early American Decoration.

and deserve mention here. There was Sidney Thomas who had a tin foot which he had manufactured carefully after an accident and an amputation. Sidney and his father, whose routes ran through Pardville and Ohio City in Herkimer

County, New York, were both smith and peddler. They traveled widely, and Sidney resoled his foot whenever it wore thin.

The peddler whom New Yorkers around Laurens knew as Briggs, was also an amputee, his losses more drastic than that of Thomas: the Otsego peddler had lost both legs at the hips. For work he adopted a unique costume—brief leather breeches and heavy leather gloves. Although he journeyed distances by wagon, in order to get from cart to house he swung his torso along at remarkable speed using arms for legs and hands for feet.

Another peddler, "Blind Cripton," of Norton, Vermont, tapped his way around neighboring townships. His sense of hearing was exceptionally keen and when he talked to children along

Stevens Plains deed box with brass lock and key. Courtesy of Bernice Drury, Springfield, Vermont.

102

his route, he could identify the family to which each child belonged. Since he had learned where families lived in relation to each other, the children were guideposts. Over the years, Cripton gained a reputation as a philosopher who relished spending his evenings in a warm farm kitchen, discussing religion, history, or medicine. His friends were happy to pick dandelion greens to please him, and they scrupulously avoided serving pork in his presence. Disdainfully, he referred to this meat as "squeal grease."

MAINE DECORATION

There were a number of tinware decorators among the Maine tin families. One of the first of these was Sarah, Tom Briscoe's wife, along with at least three of the five nieces the Briscoes adopted: Hattie, Maria and Sally Francis. *All* of the girls painted if one can trust the reminiscences printed in the *Deering News*:

> Briscoe was a pedlar and the driver of his own cart. His goods consisted of japanned tinware, japanned and ornamented by his wife, aided later by five orphaned nieces.

The known painting of Zachariah Stevens seems unique, although we must recognize that the decorators he trained were apt to develop a style much like his own. This is true in many cases where decorators worked together, hence designs are usually designated as a type done by certain painters, although not necessarily the work of that painter. Pieces of tinware decorated by Zachariah have been preserved by his descendants, and considerable research by the late Esther Stevens Brazer allows us to be certain of some characteristics of his painting. He was a master of his craft. His patterns were carefully executed—his painting imaginative and charming. On pieces done for members of the family, designs are fine and technique flawless.

The borders that he used to complement the larger pattern on a box, tray, or caddy are more complex than most, and prettier. These borders are not casual, the label which might be applied to most country-painted borders; they have an importance of their own. Fancier pieces attributed to Zachariah have borders with leaves and berries and intricate brush strokes of different colors. Sometimes, on colored backgrounds, a border resembling black rickrack is found.

The noteworthy use of color on Stevens Plains ware was mentioned at the beginning of this chapter. Besides white, yellow, and red backgrounds, black was usual. (This appears to be heavy japan paint.) Green backgrounds have been found in different sections of New England, but the ornamentation on such tinware is usually stencilled with bronze powders, not flowered.

The practice of using a white band under decoration is unusual in Maine. Motifs are more natural looking than in much country-tin decoration. I have seen shells and cornucopias on Maine-painted ware, but more common motifs are flowers, fruit, and leaves. Cherries and strawberries are popular along with other small berries, such as currants, gooseberries, or blueberries. Petaling of flowers is often intricate and fine cross-hatching represents highlights. Occasionally designs are just combinations of red and yellow with leaves blended from shades of olive green, or solid green leaves with straight black or yellow veins. Once in a while one finds blue flowers or pinks and blues blended with white into pastel shades. The blending of wet color with a brush appears to be popular with Maine painters. (Almost all other country painting is flat, painted wet-on-dry, with no blending.) The

Coffin-lid tray with white band which is rare in Maine. Collection of the author.

blue-green found on British-made and decorated pierced-edge trays and caddies is found in Maine, perhaps an indication that her early decorators were trained in Britain.

Sally, one of Tom Briscoe's adopted daughters, married Zachariah Stevens' son Samuel. Their descendants remember that Sally kept her brushes and paints on a table in the living room so that she might be ready to paint at a moment's notice. She was fond of painting roses, and Mrs. Brazer identified a bread tray with roses in the center as "Grandmother's bread tray."

Another Stevens Plains painter was tinman Oliver Buckley. Buckley was born in Connecticut in 1781, migrated to Maine to practice his trades, and lived there until his death in 1872. Oliver had two daughters, Mary Ann and Nancy, who may have painted. Mrs. Brazer labeled a particular kind of design as that of Buckley. The patterns are symmetric, and shades of color are consistent: peach, white, dark alizarin, and a green with considerable blue in it. A tray in my collection with decoration of this type is marked on the back "Brookfield 1845." A girl's name also appears, but it is not completely legible.

Maine tinmen liked a second distinctive trunk shape. (Remember the flat-topped trunks mentioned earlier in this chapter.) The difference in this second shape is also in the lid, which has two levels, one raised from the other with tinplate resembling beveling. Such shape variations as these may be used as guides toward identification. It is probably unrealistic to say that any one tinware shape belonged exclusively to one tin center.

Tinmen and painters were active in Maine for years, and a gentleman wrote that between 1800 and 1835, more of Maine's young men were graduated from tin carts than from her favorite college, Bowdoin. "And," said he, "it is believed and judged a far less proportion of all the pedlars have been failures in life than of the college graduates."

Spread of
the Tin Industry
to New York
and Vermont

*A*T THE SHELBURNE MUSEUM beside Lake
Champlain in Shelburne, Vermont, you may see
a tin peddler's wagon, full size. If you visit the
museum of The New-York Historical Society
in New York City, scour the displays until you
find the peddlers' wagons, toy size. These are
accurate, miniature replicas carved from wood,
complete with tinware hanging from racks on
top of these cupboards-on-wheels which the tin
peddler rode from farm to farm. The New York
State Historical Association museums in Cooperstown house a number of fine pieces of decorated tinware, some owned by the Association,
some by The Historical Society of Early American Decoration. Perhaps the most important features in New York State are the careful repre-
sentations of tin shops at the Shaker Museum at
Chatham and the Rochester Museum of Arts
and Sciences. There is also an exceptionally
complete display of tin tools at Old Museum
Village in Monroe, just off the lower end of the
New York Thruway.

**TINMEN IN
NEW YORK CITY**

All of the earliest tin centers were near water,
and probably this was no accident, since for

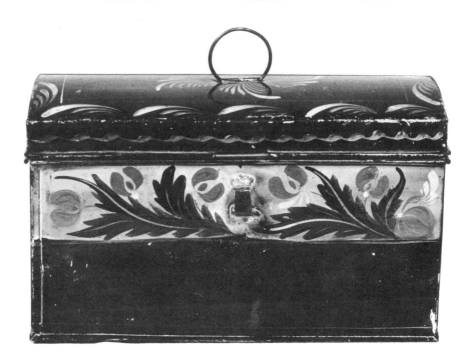

Document or deed box with simple design. Collection of the author.

many years the materials of the tinsmith were imported. Dedham is near Boston and her harbor; Stevens Plains, near Portland and the ocean; Berlin is just above Middletown on the Connecticut River.

New York City, too, made a contribution to the tin trade. Four tinsmiths with the same given name appear on early rosters. John Baltus Dash, an advertiser in the *New-York Mercury* in 1765, migrated to America from Germany to open his shop near the Oswego Market. His son John became a tinsmith, and the shop at the corner of Liberty Street and Broadway was busy for several generations, supplying wholesale and retail trades. The two Johns were active members of the German Society, influential in early New York City affairs.

Another tinman, John Graham, was working at about the same time; this is evidenced by an advertisement that appeared on April 23, 1770, in the *New-York Gazette and Weekly Mercury*:

> John Graham, Tinman, informs his friends and customers, that he is removed from the house where Mr. Baltus Dash formerly lived to the next

door but one where Mr. Whitman used to live, in the Broad-way, near the lower end of Oswego Market, where he makes and mends all sorts of tinware as usual . . . All those that will favor him with their custom, will be served at the most reasonable rates, By their most humble servant,

John Graham

Graham was listed as a tinplate worker in the 1786 Directory of New York along with Dash, Samuel Kempton, Richard Roseumen of Dock Street and William Bailey. Graham was prominent in the city militia and when he died in 1805, his wife Sarah listed among his goods "one set of tinman's tools—$50."

In 1773 an English tinman, John Burch, practiced in New York and provides an early reference to the japanning of tinware in this country. (Many of the japanners who advertised in our

Coffeepot with fine details in design. Courtesy of Frances Elliot, Saugerties, New York.

109

An Act in relation to Hawkers and Pedlers.

Passed March 23. 1840.

The people of the State of New York represented in Senate and Assembly do enact as follows:

§1. Section three of title four of chapter Seventeen of the First part of the Revised Statutes is amended so as to read as follows: "Every applicant for a Licence as a hawker or pedler before he shall be entitled to a Licence shall pay into the Treasury the following duties: If he intend to travel <u>On Foot</u> the Sum of <u>Twenty Dollars for One years Licence</u>: If he intend to travel and carry his goods with a <u>single Horse</u> or <u>other beast</u> carrying or drawing a burthen, or with a <u>Boat</u> or <u>Boats</u> the Sum of <u>Thirty Dollars for One years Licence</u>: and if he intend to travel with any vehicle or carriage drawn by <u>more than One horse</u> or other animal the Sum of <u>Fifty dollars for a years Licence</u>: which several Sums shall be reduced proportionally for any Shorter term not less than Six months.

§2 The fifth Section of the Same title and chapter is so amended as to read as follows: "Such Licences may be issued at any time for any term <u>not less than Six months</u> nor more than one year, and every Licence granted or to be granted shall be renewed on the Expiration thereof by the Secretary of State if Such renewal be applied for, on the Same terms and conditions that the Original Licence was granted."

§3. The Eighth Section of the Same title and Chapter is amended by adding to the end of the Section the following Clause: "It shall be the duty of the overseers of the poor of the Several towns of this State to Enforce the provisions of the law in the manner herein prescribed whenever any violation thereof within their respective towns shall come to their Knowledge". Compared with the Original.

first newspapers worked on furniture or carriages, not tinware.)

> John Burch, Tin-Plate Worker and Japanner, from London, has removed from the Fly, to the house on Hanover-Square lately occupied by Mr. Lloyd Dabney, and opposite Mr. Gaine's Printing-Office, where he carries on both branches in the most extensive manner. He has by him a most extensive collection of tinware of all kinds, both plain and japan'd, which he will sell as cheap as they can be bought in London. Those *who buy to sell again* will have a large allowance made them. As several parts of this business are entirely new in this country, he hopes for such encouragement as may induce him to continue them. N.B. Many block-tin articles for kitchen use, warranted to stand the fire and not have any pernicious quality, as many other metals have.

PEDDLERS' FEES REQUIRED

Over the years more and more states demanded licenses from the peddlers, many of whom "bought to sell again" as suggested by John Burch. In New York State in 1840 a peddler on foot paid twenty dollars; a peddler with one horse, thirty dollars. Two horses and a cart required payment of a fee of fifty dollars, and peddlers who rode the Erie Canal boats with their ware paid thirty dollars. Licensing requirements caused some master smiths to set up branch shops in different states and in Canada. Thus peddlers could work within a state and purchase one license instead of several. For years license fees for peddlers going into Canada were exorbitant—at one time two hundred forty dollars annually for a one-horse outfit and two hundred sixty dollars for two horses with a tin cart. It is easy to understand why the Filleys in 1817 sent John Mills and Asa French to LaPrairie, Quebec, just south of Montreal, with instructions to make, japan, and paint tinware.

1840 act regulating peddlers. Courtesy of New York State Library, Albany, New York.

AUGUSTUS FILLEY IN LANSINGBURG

The licensing laws probably also influenced Augustus Filley to cross state lines to Lansingburg, New York. (This village was incorporated into the city of Troy in 1901, comprising the northern, more residential, part of the city.) In 1810, Lansingburg was a thriving community of about three hundred buildings sheltering fifteen hundred people. There were five churches, a bank, and an academy for boys—"Tuition $45 a quarter, board may be had in good families for $1.25 per week." Young ladies were taught reading, writing, arithmetic, grammar, geography, sewing, and ornamental needlework by a certain Miss Oake. The town "taylor" was Mr. Sam Bontecou, and the town milliner, Eliza Flack. "The Friends of Liberty, Peace and Commerce" congregated at Mr. Hill's Coffee House.

Processions of teams and wagons carried produce to market in Lansingburg: grain, lumber, whiskey, cider, potash, beef, and pork. They returned home with salt, hardware, and other necessities. Near Lansingburg, at Watervliet a horse-tow ferry carried passengers and produce

Deed box with bold flowers. Courtesy of Cooper Union Museum, New York City.

Small coffin-lid tray.
Collection of the author.

back and forth across the Hudson. Ocean-going sloops sailed up the river to load and unload cargoes.

In 1811, Augustus Filley and his bride Amelia of Bloomfield, Connecticut, moved to Lansingburg to make their home and set up the tin shop which Augustus was to manage. He had teamed up with his cousin Oliver who had promised financial backing.

Trained tinmen from the Nutmeg State followed Augustus to the new shop. Usually there were apprentices, journeymen, and a decorator or two there, although the number of workmen fluctuated with the season. Smiths worked hardest during the winter and spring, making up an assortment of ware for the peddlers who began to appear in April. The services of apprentices could be bought for five dollars before 1820, and local newspapers carried ads for "boys of fourteen or fifteen from the country" to learn all sorts of trades.

Augustus boarded his apprentices and the unmarried journeymen. He bought culinary supplies in variety—beef, shad, cider, turnips, flour, and pork—and was always on the lookout for a housekeeper, a job which at one time he urged his mother to undertake. He wrote to his partner who had been trying to secure help for him, "As for Widow Marshall, I don't want her for she is too old and lonely. See about W. Brown."

The master smith was a strict taskmaster with high standards of workmanship. In November, 1815, he reported:

> I had some dispute with Larken about his work and told him plain English that as for tin being worked the way he made some of it, I would not have it. . . . I won't be tormented with bad work . . . if I clean out the whole of them.

During unsettled post-war years it was difficult to hire and keep trained men. Some were homesick for their families back in Connecticut; another journeyman was ready to leave when he heard that there were cases of smallpox in Albany. One workman drank heavily; another demanded wages Augustus thought he didn't deserve. The master was plagued by the comings and goings of the tinmen and noted:

> I would be willing Deming should come down, he pays his own expenses. Barker for a short time at $26 but not long [this is $26 a month]. . . . You need not pay his expenses for he will come if nobody pays him for he is courting a girl here.

Again, "Deming agreed to come back but he is unsteady as the wind in notions," and, finally, "The Devil begins with workmen."

From Connecticut, the Land of Steady Habits, came a few tinmen—Joseph P. Hall, Luther Brown, a Mr. Hubbard, and Asohet Goodrich

Butler bun tray with brush stroke design. Initials M. B. painted on bottom. Courtesy of James Stevens, Greenville, New York.

—who could be trusted to turn out an honest day's work. These smiths were paid $20 to $26 a month except when they worked exceptionally long hours. During one rush season Augustus mentioned, "Luther earns $40 a month and Asohet hard upon $60."

Materials for tinware sometimes proved as difficult to find as competent workmen. Some supplies were sent to Lansingburg from Oliver's shop; others were purchased locally. Tinplate was occasionally available in Troy or in Albany at T. M. Coun and Company or at A. W. Kellogg and Company. Kellogg listed among "late arrivals from Liverpool," one hundred sixty boxes of tinplate, assorted and extra sizes. In 1815, the price of a box of tinplate varied from $14 to $19.50. Filley ledgers record large payments for tin "plait" to William H. Imlay of New York City. Orders shipped from there or from Boston arrived by boat, the Hudson River providing the most practical means of transportation for years. The cousins bought for each other when it was to their advantage. On May 24, 1816, Augustus wrote:

> As for tin, I want some sent as soon as possible for I have borrowed 18 boxes and can't borrow any more and shall have to pay $19 cash for all that I can get here and I am out of money. Send the tin – a few boxes by Troy sloop and agree on price per box.

Later he explained:

> Today I received 11 boxes of that tin. It is at Rhinebeck & I shall write and have the rest of it stored there for the Captain sent it by some men and they charged me $1.00 per hundred for fetching it & I will have the rest stored until I can get it up some cheaper.

Pattern on deed box similar to those attributed to Filleys. Note bold brush strokes on top. Courtesy of James Stevens, Greenville, New York.

Wire, too, could usually be found in Albany, although sometimes Augustus sent to the Connecticut shop for special sizes.

> I bought small sizes of wire 17-18-19 cents per pound, English wire in Albany, but none more to be had up there. . . . I expect if you can spare me some of yours from Boston it would be best to send me some.

Augustus depended on Oliver for other supplies, for example, rivets and Whitfield Patent Ears for buckets.

It was a problem to get turpentine for japan paint at a sensible price: $1.25 per gallon was too much. Consequently this varnish was often concocted at Oliver's and carted in barrels to Lansingburg. The gay oil paints used by decorators were available in Albany and Troy so that Augustus frequently sent these back to Connecticut. A letter notes, "As for vermilion, I shall send you four pound by mail." Account books itemized the purchases of chrome and King's yellow and white "led." Gale and Thompson's in Lansingburg sold Prussian blue and Chinese vermilion: $23.10 for eleven pounds, two ounces of the latter.

Tin shops found it profitable to stock sundries for their peddlers. An 1818 Filley inventory lists one hundred dollars' worth of buttons, combs, hooks, and "things on hand." The last category probably included scissors, thimbles, buckles, fish hooks, and jackknives.

The peddlers kept Augustus busy; they are mentioned frequently in his reports to Oliver:

> I have a bill of about $700 to make out next week and two pedlars waiting now.

> If I had had last week and the week before $4200 worth of tin I would have sold it. We have worked 72 boxes here.

Barnes and Noble got here last night and want tin this summer.

Mills has been here and wants Japan tin.

The Filleys loaded peddlers who traded chiefly in eastern New York, in Vermont, and in Canada. Filley letters refer to these traveling salesmen: Hial Holcomb, John Mills, Russell Phillips, Hial Fuller, G. Adams, Seth Holt, Warren Adams, and a Mr. Dunbar. In December, 1816, Augustus passed on gossip of conditions in Canada:

> I have a letter from Mr. G. Adams, Canada, & he says not far from the first or 10th of March he shall be in and he has done well and some buttons and some combs he shall want & two heavy loads of tin and then I shall have some money. The talk in Canada is of doubling the license but he will pay and peddle another year.

In another letter is this comment:

> As for peddlers in the upper Provinces of Canada, they, I think, will do pretty well, those that are acquainted, but it will not do to send greenhorns in the lower Provinces. They may do something but Money is scarce.

Despite this scarcity of hard money, Augustus commented later in 1816, "Uncle Warren Adams cleared $165 over his ware this trip."

As barter piled up Augustus notified his partner: "I have got on hand 500 muskrat skins and want to know what you can get there in Hartford for them"; "I have four or five hundredweight of feathers and about the same of old pewter"; "I want to know if tow cloth, yard wide, will sell there." Coarse wool, and pairs of mittens lined with flannel are also mentioned. Since Lansingburg and Troy were headquarters for peddlers, almost any barter they brought

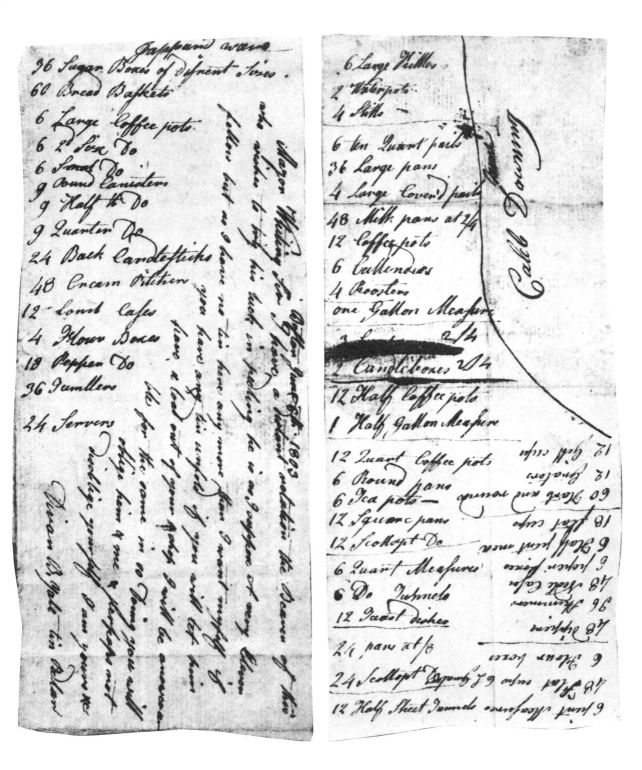

Tin peddler's list from back of Vivian Yale note. Courtesy of Baker Library, Harvard University, Cambridge, Massachusetts.

in could find a buyer. The *Lansingburg Gazette* advertised:

> Cash and a generous price paid for tanned Sheep Skins suitable for book-binding, at the Lansingburg Book Store.

> Alexander Walsh—the highest prices will be given for Martin, Mink, Fox and Fisher Skins.

> Cash and the highest prices for clean cotton and linen RAGS, at the Lansingburg Book Store by Tracy and Bliss.

> Mustard Seed—Cash paid for any quantity of MUSTARD SEED by Lansing and Alvord.

Local stores catered to the peddlers in more ways than one. A. Walsh advertised that he had for sale three hundred gross of very cheap buttons. S. Freiot and Company, whose motto was "A nimble sixpence is worth a slow shilling," inserted this ad: "Country merchants & Pedlars are requested to call, as they will find Goods at the above Store very low." Peddlers Rens Wray and James Guild from upper New York and western Vermont, respectively, stocked up

Tray and colander made by Niskayuna Shakers. Collection of the author.

on tinware and sundries in Lansingburg and Troy, twin headstones mark the burial places

There were Filley tinshops in Lansingburg for years, guided by the men (and women) of several generations. Edwin followed his father, Augustus, and as late as 1879 a tin and hardware shop listed its proprietor as Mrs. George Filley. Augustus himself lived until 1846, busy at his trade, and, like Uncle Zach Stevens, in politics. A Whig, he acted as a justice of the peace, sheriff, and member of the state legislature. Today, at the top of a knoll in Oakwood Cemetery, Troy, twin headstones mark the burial places of Augustus and Amelia, and the name of Filley is prominent still in the community.

THE SHAKERS

It may seem queer to consider a whole community as a family, yet the Shakers considered themselves such. Before describing their tinware, it seems necessary to review the background of these people whose beliefs and way of life affected the way they worked and the products they made.

The first colony of Believers in the Second Appearing of Christ [Shaker is a contraction of Shaking Quakers, a name applied to the sect by nonmembers] settled in Niskayuna, New York, near the present Albany Airport, in 1776. The original group which migrated from the vicinity of Manchester, England, was made up of eight men and women who came over on the ship *Mariah*. Their leader was Ann Lee, a blue-eyed, solemn-looking girl, the daughter of a blacksmith. It was Ann Lee, a partner in an unhappy marriage, who drew up the chief tenets of the group, the first of which was celibacy. Other requirements were confession of sins, community of goods, and withdrawal from the world.

Shaker buildings, Niskayuna Colony, near present airport, Albany, New York.

Only supreme effort and Ann's inspiration kept the original group from abandoning their colony in a swampy, overgrown wilderness. Mother Ann's oft-repeated maxim "Put your hands to work and your hearts to God" was no idle principle. Rough log structures were erected by the eight, and they went out as missionaries to convert their neighbors to their precepts.

Everything members of the sect (which soon grew to be thousands strong) did, was according to a pattern set by Ann Lee and subsequent elders and eldresses. The Millennial Laws, recorded in 1821, laid down rules governing all phases of life. Simplicity was the keynote in Shaker living. Individuals strove to be humble and to work for the good of all. Their aims are expressed in their hymn, "The Rock."

> I want to feel little,
> I want to feel small,
> The last of my brethren,
> The least of them all.
>
> I want to feel humble,
> And simple in mind,
> More watchful, more careful,
> More fully resigned.
>
> I want to be holy,
> More perfect in love,
> I want to be gentle
> And meek as a dove.

Most Shakers were hard-working folk. Sam Steele, a tinker from Catskill, New York, had spent several months in the Niskayuna Shaker community when the brethren finally asked him to leave. He explained afterward that they had accused him of taking so long to hoe a row of corn that the shade from his borrowed broad-brimmed hat had killed the plants! At any rate the tinker was ready to return to Catskill and his trade; sleeping near the Mohawk flats and drinking only cold water had "caused the frogs to croak in my belly," he said.

"Do all your work as if you had a thousand years to live, and live as though you were going to die tomorrow," was a motto which had a particularly noticeable effect upon crafts and craftsmen. The elders also preached, "If you improve one talent, God will give you more," and they set out to prove this. All the members rotated in their jobs—the women, for example, working in the kitchen one month, in the weaving room the next. Henry DeWitt, a Canadian

Shaker lamp filler. Collection of the author.

who joined the Niskayuna group in 1815, kept
a journal and wrote:

> Sometimes a-fixing spinning wheels
> At other times to work on reels;
> If I should mention all I do;
> My time and paper would be few.
>
> And so it is while time does last,
> I find enough to do;
> With busy hands can't work so fast
> But what there's more to do.

Brother DeWitt mentions cutting trees, plowing,
laying stone walls, haying, making clothespins,
and working as a tinsmith. Elder Harvey Eads
of South Union, Kentucky, was a shoemaker,
teamster, seed-grower, tailor, book-binder, wool-
carder, dentist, spinner, printer, hatter, author,
and bishop, and tin and sheet-iron worker.

The Shaker sect was thriving at a time when
tin utensils were found in every household. Since
these people were taught not to depend on "the
World," they made for themselves quantities
of tinware as well as other necessities. According to the Wells sisters, who lived in the Niskayuna Community as late as 1940, their sect also
made tinware to sell. The study of this ware is
not the study of individual smiths and their
work, but rather the study of the sect—many
members of which knew the tinners' trade—
along with examples of their unusually perfect
ware.

Labor of every sort among the Shakers was
anonymous; each task was performed for the
sake of the cause rather than for personal satis-
faction. No pieces were marked so that they
might be identified as the work of an individual.
Each piece of tinware, as well as each chair, each
yard of Shaker-woven material, each packet of
herbs, was as perfect as the workman could
produce.

Shaker teapot. Courtesy of the New York State Historical Association, Cooperstown, New York.

The Shaker tinsmith manufactured unusual items for special purposes: bobbins used in weaving, a steam pot for use in preparing straw for hats or rush for seat bottoms, a candleholder to clip on a book. This creation of unusual pieces was typical of the Shakers. Their chair-makers constructed heavy, reinforced chairs for fat deacons and a contraption to lift an ailing sister from her bed.

A piece of tinplate became a pattern for the first circular saw; this was designed by a Shaker woman, Tabitha Babbitt. Here is the account of a Harvard, Massachusetts, resident:

> One day as she was spinning, she noticed the brethren sawing wood in the old-fashioned way; she observed that one-half of the motion was lost, and so conceived the idea of the circular saw. She made a tin disc, notched it around the edge, slipped it on the spindle of her wheel, tried it out on a piece of shingle, found it would cut, and gave to the world the buzz saw.

Working conditions among these people were ideal. During the latter days of active Shaker history the people of "the World" vied with

Shaker pans and syrup jug.
Collection of William
Lassiter, Albany, New York.

each other for the opportunity to work in Shaker industries. Although everyone had to work hard, heat and light in Shaker factories were good. Food, although eaten in complete silence at Shaker tables, was wholesome and plentiful. Each shop was spotless, and tools were in finest condition. "Only fools drop their tools" was probably a favorite maxim.

In Shaker tinware as well as in their architecture, their clothing, and their furniture, nothing was superfluous. Although tinware was not painted or decorated, the esthetic appeal of such homely pieces as candleholders and teakettles is surprising. Marguerite Melcher, in *The Shaker Adventure*, comments:

> The only kind of beauty tolerated was that springing unsought from what is today called functionalism. For in spite of themselves, the Shakers produced things of beauty. They never tried to do so . . . it was a by-product not of their planning.

126

The Believers were expressly forbidden to make or own ornamented tinware. Their Millennial Law, under Superfluities Not Owned, listed marbelized tinware—along with silver pens, silver spoons, three-bladed knives, flowery-painted clocks, gay silk handkerchiefs, and green veils. Shaker tinware is beautiful because of its simplicity of line and its lack of adornment. It is also to be admired because it was made so precisely. Solder was neatly applied and smoothed. Edges were accurately cut and carefully turned. There were no sharp or rough ends. If a piece of tin were to be round, it was exact. Patterns on tin, punched or pierced for some utilitarian purpose, never merely for ornament, were usually geometric and painstakingly accurate. Handles were graceful and finials were dainty. The ware of the Shaker tinmen possessed a perfection and grace equalled by few tinsmiths of "the World."

Bun tray typical of the Butlers. Courtesy of Frances Elliot, Saugerties, New York.

AARON BUTLER AND HIS "TIN FAMILY"

Eastern New York was the home of another tin family. In 1799, Abel Butler, his wife, and their children—Samuel, Abel, Moses, Aaron, Lydia, Millie, and Hannah—packed "body, boots and britches" into an oxcart and moved from their home in Connecticut to East Greenville, northeastern Greene County, New York. The first Butler ancestor to come to America had arrived in 1633, settling in Connecticut. Several generations later, when there was no longer elbow room, Abel, with hundreds of other New Englanders, went west to New York State where he purchased a large square of land and prepared to farm it and to raise his family.

The Butlers' first home was a log house on the brow of a hill. As the Butlers tilled their acres spreading over a rolling countryside, the community of Greenville grew. Dr. Jonathan Prosser and Dr. John Bly came to settle, and Old Brownie began to ride the mail circuit. Buel

Deed box with streamlined yellow bird that resembles work of the Butlers. Courtesy of Ruby Rounds, Cooperstown, New York.

(Above) Bun tray with Butler tulip. Courtesy of James Stevens, Greenville, New York. (Below) Deed box with typical Butler tulip, flower, bud, and leaf treatment. Collection of the author.

129

(Above) Peddler John Miller and Decorator Minerva Butler Miller. Portraits courtesy of Mrs. Theodore Whitbeck, Albany, New York. (Below) Butler box with unusual primitive basket. Courtesy of Mrs. Howard Adriance, Greenville, New York.

Butler deed box. Note "dot" flowers along stems. Courtesy of James Stevens, Greenville, New York.

Cheritree set up a blacksmith shop; Levi Callendar opened a store and Isaac Hallock, a hotel. Reverend Eleazor Hodgkins' son became the first schoolmaster.

In time the Butlers prospered, and as the boys reached manhood each learned a trade. Aaron was sent back to Connecticut, apprenticed to a tinsmith. After finishing his training he returned home to marry Sarah Cornell from nearby Amenia in Dutchess County. They set up housekeeping in Greenville, soon nicknamed Brandy Hill. (One of Aaron's interests was a cider brandy distillery.) Sarah and Aaron had eleven children in all: first Ann, born in 1813, then Abel, Lewis, Hiram, Marilla, and Minerva, the latter born in 1821. In 1823, Aaron, Sarah, and their brood moved into the big white house which still stands on top of Brandy Hill. Over the next few years Harriet, Aaron, Jr., Barnum, Eliza, and young Sarah joined the family.

In 1824, Aaron opened both his tin shop and his general store. After finishing Greenville Academy his sons worked for him in the tin shop or in another of his enterprises. He operated a hay-press, a cider mill, the brandy distillery, a decorating shop, a peddling business, and his farm.

Probably all of the Butler girls were taught to paint tinware. Ann, however, was most active according to Mrs. Theodore Whitbeck, her grandniece. Ann often went on trips with her father to New York City or to nearby towns where he traded. In 1835, though, Ann married Eli Scutt, a Livingstonville farmer, and left the bustle of the home farm. As a housewife Ann had little time to paint. She used tinware from her father's shop and hung framed, painted designs on the walls of her home. Young Aaron

Bread tray with simple design by Butler. Courtesy of James Stevens, Greenville, New York.

132

Unusual Butler box. Note treatment of leaves typical of Butlers. Courtesy of Mrs. Howard Adriance, Greenville, New York.

was her firstborn, in 1840. Frank and Adelade followed. Mrs. Whitbeck recalls visits to her Aunt Ann and Uncle Eli, especially riding behind a team of oxen while her uncle drew wood from his woodlot.

At one time Aaron sent out six peddlers with carts; one of the peddlers was John Miller, an immigrant from Strasbourg, Germany. John and some friends, seeking adventure and escape from military service, had used the college tuition fees their parents sent to buy their passages to America. Once in the United States, John journeyed up the Hudson, perhaps to Saugerties, a German settlement. When he was employed by the master smith, the young peddler started courting his boss's daughter Minerva; they were married in 1843. Miller was master of the peddling business for many years. In 1859, when Aaron closed the tin shop because of his failing health, the peddler bought a corner of land from his father-in-law, built a new home for his wife

One of few Butler trays identified. Courtesy of Mrs. Maxwell Palmer, Greenville, New York.

and their children, Sarah and Marilla, and became a farmer.

In 1860, Aaron died and Butler contributions to tinsmithing ceased. One can still see a marble monument marking Aaron's grave in the burying ground behind the family home, and we recall the sentiments of Minerva, carefully penned in an album:

> Remember me is all I ask
> And if remembrance be a task,
> Forget me.

THE NORTHS OF FLY CREEK

Stephen North, the fifth son of Jedediah North, Connecticut toolmaker, was born in 1767 and married in 1788. At some point he learned the tinsmithing trade and, according to a family genealogy "early removed to western New York." Actually Stephen and his family established themselves in Fly Creek, northwest of Cooperstown, New York (just over a hill and down into a wide valley), sometime between 1790, when records show that they were still in Berlin, and 1800, by which time they had settled in Fly Creek.

Stephen's bride was Susannah Savage, daughter of a Revolutionary War soldier. Perhaps she learned tin painting in Berlin and later taught it to her daughters, for it was a piece of tinware with Mercy's name on it that led backward to the family of North tinmen. The Stephen Norths had a large family. Albert, the oldest child, was born in 1789 in Connecticut; others followed at brief intervals: Emily, Linus, Almira, Mercy, Stephen, Hepzibah, Susan, and Orrin. About the elder Stephen a church paper noted: "In closing his business he left no other legacy to his children than the instructions they had received during his lifetime." The gentleman who recorded this note added, "How much better than any pecuniary legacy he might have left them."

North document box.
Courtesy of Emily Heath, Thetford, Vermont.

The two oldest of Stephen's sons became tin-smiths. Between 1820 and 1850, Albert advertised frequently in a Cooperstown newspaper, *The Freeman's Journal.* These advertisements advised the public that they might purchase tin-ware at the shop on Turnpike Road. Albert also wrote regularly to his cousin Jedediah in Connecticut concerning business. Both were grandsons of the Jedediah North who had founded the tool-making business and who died in 1816. Albert's letters were sometimes gossipy with family affairs, sometimes completely businesslike. like.

> Fly Creek
> July 1, 1822
>
> Dear Jedediah,
>
> I have wrote to Orrin Beckley to procure for me a set of machine tools for working tin-ware which I expect will cost something more than a hundred dollars. Whatever the amount I wish you to pay it to Orrin Beckley when he calls for it according to an arrangement between your sister Lucy and myself. She wanted the money to get things to start keeping house. I did not know how to get it until I proposed to furnish the tools and pay her here. Lucy is mar-ried and all parties appear to be happy in the connection. We all enjoy comfortable health. Almira's health is improving.
>
> Yours respectfully,
> Albert North

Linus North started out to become a preacher but ill health, resulting in at least temporary loss of his voice, deterred him. Later he, too, turned tinsmith. One of his letters has to do with an order for tools:

> November, 1822
>
> Dear Sir –
>
> I rec'd your letter on the subject of tinsmith's tools and should have written to you immedi-ately but I was under the necessity of delaying

Fronts and ends of deed boxes attributed to Norths of Fly Creek, New York. Box on left has vermillion band. Collection of the author. Box on right has white band. Courtesy of the New York State Historical Association, Cooperstown, New York.

for some circumstances which I could not avoid. I can now inform you of what I am in want. I wish for one set of tinsmith's tools with the exception of a large stake which you will recollect I have received via Savage but in the place of a large stake I wish you would add a large pair of shears for sheet iron work. From the pin let the blades be nine inches long. Let the bars be two feet, stiff and stout. Brother Albert also wishes you to send him a pr. of shears. He wishes them to be one side stouter than common tin. I wish the tools to be sent by water to Albany in case you can send them before the water closes. . . . Our time is short but I hope you will make an effort to send them in time not to be stopped by ice through the winter. I wish immediate use of the tools. You will please to send the bill for the tools by mail and I will endeavor to find a chance to send you the money by mail. Put the tools in a good box so they can not dent. Mark the box so it will not rub off. Send it to the care of Trotter and Douglas, Albany, New York, for Albert North, Otsego. Your friends here all in good health. Give my respects to your father and mother, to your wife and to all friends.

Your friend,
Linus North

A letter written from Palmyra, New York, during the next year explains further:

I am establishing a shop for tin, sheet-iron and Patent combs in connection with one of my brothers-in-law. This place promises a good support for the business.

Bread tray with faint inscription "Mercy North" on floor. Courtesy of the New York State Historical Association, Cooperstown, New York.

Business did prosper, and although plagued by ill health, Linus lived until 1846 and the age of fifty-two.

At least two of Albert's sons, Stephen and Ceylon, followed the family trade. Stephen married and moved to Jonesville, Michigan, where he was identified by the dignified title "tin and iron mechanic." Ceylon shared his father's business in Fly Creek until 1841 when the older man retired.

Presbyterian Church records offer information about the Norths, a church family which produced innumerable missionaries, deacons, elders, and teachers of religion. They belonged at first to the Presbyterian Church in Cooperstown, joining when it was founded in 1800. By 1828 they had helped to build a church in Fly Creek.

The home of the Norths still stands, what a realtor would call a two-story Colonial, now painted white and standing cater-corner from the Sportsmen's Tavern. A wagonshed is attached to one side of the house, perhaps a shelter for tin carts in earlier days. In back of the house is a small red building, what is left of Stephen and Albert's store. Above the entrance swings a door through which produce or barter could be raised and stored. Inside the building, vestiges of hair plaster cling to the walls and the beams are lined with cut nails and pegs from which merchandise was hung.

DECORATION IN NEW YORK STATE

We do not know for certain that any of the womenfolk in Stephen North's household could paint, although it is probable that several of them could. Mercy may not have been the decorator who painted her name in spidery script across the floor of a bread tray owned by the New York State Historical Association at Cooperstown. As a matter of fact, there were two Mercy Norths who were contemporaries, the second the wife of Norris, a tinsmith, who lived in Elmira, New York.

We are sure that there were decorators in Jedediah's family in Berlin. Albert North wrote from Fly Creek to suggest that Jedediah send "one of his sisters" to Fly Creek to work; there were eight sisters—Patty, Lucy, Sarah, Beulah, Rachel, Marilla, Olive, and Julia. From the letter one would infer that all of them were painters. When Albert issued the invitation he wrote, "I think that I can occupy her Leisure hours at Painting." (From correspondence mentioned previously, it is obvious that at least Lucy visited the Fly Creek family, for she married and settled there.) In ledgers recording expenditures of North tinmen, Betsey North is listed frequently on payrolls. (This was the name of Jedediah's wife and also of one of their daughters.)

The Mercy North tray has a hallmark to de-

139

light anyone investigating antiques: a distinctive mottled background. This looks as if heavy japan paint had been applied with the end of a one-inch sash brush in a regular pattern on an already dry coat of thinner japan paint. The design on this piece is also distinctive. On the floor there is a repeat border of white brush-stroke flowers with vermilion overstrokes, alternating with green brush-stroke leaves which follow graceful vermilion stems. On the outside edge of the tray a similar border surmounts a white band. The flowers on this are vermilion with alizarin overstrokes, and the leaves have fine yellow lines as accents. There is also a brush-stroke border beneath the white band. Almost identical designs have been observed on bun trays, caddies, match holders, a teapot, and deed boxes. Sometimes the band is red instead of white and a rope border with "dot" flowers is used. Tops of boxes

Large deed box with profusion of fine details. Courtesy of Ione Robertson, Glens Falls, New York.

(Left) Small caddy. Courtesy of the New York State Historical Association, Cooperstown, New York. (Right) Unusual horn with painting. Collection of the author.

have brush-stroke motifs like others except for one striking difference. Such designs are usually all yellow but the tops of North boxes have vermilion strokes complete with overstrokes, *plus* green and yellow strokes.

North patterns are related to those found in Connecticut. Their decoration is professionally expert. Usual country-tin colors are used: red vermilion, medium green, chrome yellow, aliz-

(Above) Small trinket box. (Below) Initials of Ann Butler on back of box. Courtesy of Mrs. Howard Adriance, Greenville, New York.

arin crimson, and white. In this type of North
pattern which we are able to identify, the pattern is made up of a series of well-balanced repeat borders.

Some of New York's most charming decorated ware can be attributed to the Butler girls
who have left similar pieces, some signed with
full names ("Ann Butler") and some with initials ("A.B.," "M.B.," "H.B.,"). An autograph
album belonging to Minerva is illustrated with
the same sort of patterns that the girls used on
tinware. They often used white bands under
borders although their borders are unlike those
from other shops. Designs are busy; Ann and
her sisters seemed to feel obligated to fill each
bare spot with a zigzag line, dot, brush-stroke,
or star-shaped flower. Cross-hatching of fine lines
was used to highlight.

Flowers, leaves, and geometric motifs are
found most often on Butler tinware. The flowers
are roses, full-blown or in bud, or tulips, or one
of three or four unidentifiable brush-stroke blossoms. Simplifications of these patterns—a spray
of rosebuds, a single tulip, or brush-stroke flower
—are found on small pieces, such as caddies or
bread trays. These simpler pieces are thought
to be the family's quickly done, highly commercial ware. Geometric motifs, used on box
tops or ends or on small trays, are sometimes
feathery tracings and sometimes bold designs in
yellow. Leaves are oval, with a light side and
a dark side and either black or yellow veins; or,
they are elongated like elm leaves with fine curving veins; or, they are indicated by multiple fine
brush strokes along stems that are unusually
slender.

Colors used are significant. The red is not
orangy, and greens vary from dark yellow-green

Deed box from Vermont-
New York border. Courtesy
of Mrs. George Pierce,
Easton, New York.

(Left) Bread tray which
would hold old-time sliced
loaf. Courtesy of Frances
Elliot, Saugerties, New York.
(Right) Deed box. See
drawer-pull handle. Courtesy
of James Stevens, Greenville,
New York.

to emerald. Yellows are apt to have white in
them. Prussian blue is found once in a while.
Alizarin and white overstrokes are finer than
ordinary. All-in-all, the Butler designs are well
balanced and the busyness of the fancier ware
creates a special charm and a unique appearance.

So far two types of decoration found in New
York State and its vicinity have been neglected.
Whether or not these types originated in shops
already familiar is unknown. One kind of pattern

is found along the northeastern part of the state where it borders Vermont. Along this route Filley peddlers traveled to Canada; "Honest" Wilson of Barre, Vermont, and Noyes' peddlers from Burlington, bartered their ware. The unique feature of this tinware is its color combination: vermilion, dark blue-green, white, Prussian blue, and yellow. Brush-stroke flowers and natural-looking leaves make up the motifs. Usually there is a blending of white and blue on a vermilion flower, and brush strokes that conventionally are yellow, are white. Striping, which is profuse, may be red, blue, or white, or a combination of all three. The japanned background is not black but bronze or honey-color.

Another type of pattern found in quantities in New York has bold patterns, usually covering the piece almost completely. Motifs are made up of brush-stroke flowers and leaves, expertly, although sometimes hastily, applied. The painting has a particularly professional look about it. These designs appear on every kind of country

Deed box with wet-on-wet blending typical of painted tinware found along Vermont-New York border. Courtesy of James Stevens, Greenville, New York.

145

tin and probably originated in one of the already familiar shops, that of the Filleys, the Butlers, or the Norths, although I have never seen a piece which had any sort of significant identification.

Tinmen
and Peddlers
in Pennsylvania
and Farther West

$\mathcal{P}$ENNSYLVANIA is a romantic state. Even a casual trip through east-central Pennsylvania today reminds one that this is true. In the communities of the Mennonites, the Amish, and the River Brethren, the men in their black suits and broad-brimmed hats, neatly aproned and bonnetted women in long dresses, and children who are miniatures of their parents, appear to be figures transplanted from another age.

The state is beloved by antiquarians for Pennsylvanians are "savers." Antique shops are plentiful and well stocked; so are the museums. There is more tinware in the Philadelphia Museum of Fine Arts and the State Museums at Harrisburg, Sunbury, and Landis Valley than I have seen in collections in any other state. (There is also a fine collection of tinware at the Henry Francis Dupont Winterthur Museum at Winterthur, near Wilmington, Delaware. Much of this tinware is of the type identified with Pennsylvania.)

The most charming peddler tale I know, if one can call a tale of murder "charming," originated along Pennsylvania's Schuylkill River.

Here in the late 1700s, strange phenomena occurred. Under a tall pine on a bank high above the river, snow melted in the wintertime. In spring and summer, no grass or flowers grew. Travelers were frightened by a shadowy figure which, like a dog chasing his tail, ran around and around a tree. Residents of the vicinity recounted the story of a German peddler who had been assaulted and murdered as he walked along the river with his pack on his back. When his body was discovered, rifled pack beside it, he was buried where he had fallen. The local people suspected a witch doctor who lived nearby, especially after he told a weird tale. The conjurer confessed that he had known of a man who was butchered with an axe after running around a tall pine, begging his tormenter not to kill him, threatening, "You will be found out. You will hang. If in no other way, the chickens will dig the news out of the ground." In time the suspect hanged himself; the peddler's bones were uncovered and moved to hallowed ground in a churchyard. Chickens scratched beneath the tree, new grass grew thick and, as his prediction came true, the ghostly peddler lay still.

Another story of an early peddler emanates from Pennsylvania Dutchland. Monsieur de Benneville, one of the many Europeans to write about his travels in America during the eighteenth and nineteenth centuries, told of being in Pennsylvania in 1782. The Frenchman, traveling along Old York Road, was the first to come upon a peddler who had slipped while attempting to ford the Wingahocking River. Lying in the water, he was pinned down by his heavy pack. Unable to rise, he was able only to keep his head above water, turtle fashion. M. de Ben-

Coffin-lid tray with pattern typical of tinware found in Pennsylvania. Courtesy of H. F. Du Pont Winterthur Museum, Winterthur, Delaware.

neville righted the peddler and recorded the rescue.

Mike Beasom illustrates the evolution of the tin peddler's transportation. He was a smith and peddler working in and out of a shop in Turkey Valley, twice a year circling to cover his routes. First he carried a pack and most folks placed orders to be filled by the next trip. After a few trips, customers saw Mike walking down the road pulling a two-wheeled cart "neatly constructed" and painted flame red. The cart had several compartments behind two doors fastened with hasps and padlocks. There were shafts between which Mike stood to pull his vehicle. Mike regaled the children along his route with tall stories about his team, Jim and John, the names he gave his high-topped boots. Jim was not as sure-footed as John; John was obstreperous and had to be kept under tight rein.

On a certain evening Mike stayed overnight

(Right) Deed box. (Left) Small caddy. Courtesy of the Philadelphia Museum of Art, Philadelphia, Pennsylvania.

PENNSYLVANIA SMITHS

at a familiar farm home. After he had pulled off his boots and set them in a corner, praising them as a farmer would a loyal team, Mike retired. The hired man brought in a bucket of oats from the barn and stealthily "fed" Mike's "horses." In the morning the peddler tried to thrust his feet into boots filled with grain!

Because of his good nature and his skill as a smith, Mike did well in the valley and soon graduated to a yellow one-horse cart with his name in bold letters on each side. After a while two handsome horses pulled a larger, brightly painted wagon chockful of tinware.

Pennsylvania had its share of pioneer tinsmiths. Records mention "tinn men" in Chester County as early as 1764. Berks County documents for 1757 list Henry Degenhardt as a practicing tinsmith in Reading; in 1765, Conrad Babb was also a tinsmith there. The Shades, living along Tulpehocken (or Land of Turtles) Brook, became smiths. The household account books of

George Washington for 1793-1797 show a bill paid to P. Shade. Many Berks County artisans, including the Shades, punched and pierced some of their tinware and occasionally dated their pieces.

William Bailey's advertisement in the *Carlisle Gazette* of July 25, 1792, hints at a network of thriving shops:

> William Bailey, Coppersmith of the Borough of York, Takes this method to inform the public in general and his numerous customers in particular, that he carries on the COPPERSMITHING BUSINESS, in all its various branches, as usual, at his dwelling house, opposite Mr. Andrew Johnson's Tavern, sign of the Cub and Bear. At CHAMBERSBURGH, under the direction of his son, William, at HAGERSTOWN, next door to Mr. Jacob Harry, Hatter, in partnership with his son-in-law, Mr. William Reynolds, and at FREDERICK-TOWN, near the Poor-house, in partnership with his brother-in-law, Mr. Robert McCulley. . . .
>
> He also carries on the TIN-PLATE BUSINESS, in all its various branches, at each of the

Tray in red with gray, black, and white design. Courtesy of H. F. Du Pont Winterthur Museum, Winterthur, Delaware.

above-mentioned places. He will also attend on Wednesday and Thursday in every quarterly Court Week, at Mr. THOMAS FOSTER'S in the Borough of Carlisle, in order to save his customers trouble and expense, who wish to agree for Copper or Tin Ware to be made at any of the above-mentioned places. . . .

He returns his sincere thanks to all his former customers, and hopes the continuance of their favours.

In 1796, ten master smiths in Philadelphia organized, agreed upon wages to be paid for piecework and printed a booklet listing these wages. For making one dozen gallon coffeepots of doubleweight tinplate, a smith was to receive 11 shillings, 3 pence; for a dozen wired ladles, he received 7 shillings, 6 pence. The labor on 12 large candlesticks was also worth 7 shillings, 6 pence; the labor on twelve large punched lanterns was valued at 10 shillings. One extra shilling was permitted the smith who attached

(Left) Low caddy. Collection of the author. (Right) Small tea caddy. Courtesy of Emily Heath, Thetford, Vermont.

handles to his pudding pans. The master smiths who signed this agreement were: James Truman, Joseph Baker, Jacob Raiser, Joseph Finchour, George Tryon, Malcolm Wright, Francis Graham, Thomas Bradley, Thomas Passmore, and Conrad Keller.

A Philadelphia tinshop which remained prominent for years was founded by Passmore and Samuel Williams in 1796. These tinmen offered "planished" ware, a variant of ordinary tinware. The process for making this is described in the words of the makers:

> This ware is made by repeated hammering of the ordinary tinplate upon highly polished anvils by hammers also highly polished. This condenses the grain or fiber of the tin, and renders it capable of a high polish and at the same time improves its quality.

Williams and Passmore appealed to a wholesale trade, boasting that their shop was "exceedingly well provided with facilities for executing orders expeditiously." Their advertisements also claimed, for what it was worth, that they had "furnished with culinary utensils some of the first class hotels of New York and the largest steam boats in the western waters."

Conrad Keller, operating a busy shop in 1800, lived up to the philosophy of the Puritans and Quakers who believed that a good man was a hard-working man. An indefatigable worker himself, Keller tried to light the spark of industry in each of his apprentices, sending them to their cellar workshop before sun-up to spend a long, tedious day at their benches. Apparently some of his disciples rebelled, for mention is made of attempts at chastisement which the tinsmith invariably preceded by taking a pinch of snuff. Then, as Keller coughed and sneezed,

JACOB EICHOLTZ

shouting, "Sol I cutt-ee, oder sol I hau-ee?" ("Shall I whip or flay you?") the culprit wiggled out of his grasp and evaded the punishment.

Lancaster, another of Pennsylvania's early settled towns, was the home of Jacob Eicholtz who is known as a painter of portraits and landscapes. Jacob was born during the Revolutionary War and as a teen-ager was apprenticed to his uncle, a tin- and coppersmith. How expert a smith Jacob became might be questioned, for he spent part of his time sketching portraits of his fellow apprentices on the shop walls with the charcoal that should have been heating his soldering iron. For years, however, the trade supported him and his growing family. He noted, "About this time I had a family of three or four children and yet had not the courage to relinquish the smith and become the painter."

The daybook of Eicholtz is in the library of the Historical Society of Pennsylvania in Philadelphia. The book covers the years between 1805 and 1817. First entries have to do with

Bread tray in mint condition. Courtesy of H. F. Du Pont Winterthur Museum, Winterthur, Delaware.

tinsmithing only. For instance, Martin Miller bought a tin lantern for 7 shillings, 6 pence, and had his "candlemole" mended. Soon after that there are entries charged to the State of Pennsylvania: 6 sand boxes, an oil pot, the mending of a lantern, and some candlesticks. On September 5, 1809, there is a notation, "John Reitz came to work for me." In 1811, Samuel Davis was employed at the Eicholtz shop.

By this time, entries that have to do with tinware—either sales of ware or mending jobs, which were frequent—are interspersed with such items as "Widow Cochrane, to painting male profile—7 shillings, 6 pence," "to painting a Free Mason's Apron—1 pound, 17 shillings, 6 pence." There are other notes concerning the gilding of frames, the painting of cornices, and the lettering of signboards, alongside charges for mending sausage-stuffers and tin cutters and the sale of such tinware as one sucking bottle—1 shilling, 3 pence.

Rare painted candleholder. Courtesy of H. F. Du Pont Winterthur Museum, Winterthur, Delaware.

In 1812, Eicholtz had had enough of tinsmithing and a note about which we can only sur-

155

mise, since parts of it are illegible, appears: "My . . . has taken the concerns of my business to . . . self on the 18 June 1812." A simple inventory lists: tin—$116; wire—$18; lead—$5; scale beams—$4; total—$143.

Expenditures for a painting room are itemized. The total for lime, stones, hauling, shingles, tin, and the services of a mason and of a carpenter, reached $196.85. During 1812, Eicholtz went to Boston briefly to study with Gilbert Stuart. He soon returned to Lancaster where he remained until his death in 1842.

There were three tinsmiths in Pittsburgh in 1815: John Horn of Ferry Street, William Kepner of Market Street, and James Kirtland of Diamond Alley. The number seems small for a city which had appealed to trained men in its *Gazette:* "This country offers at present the most unabounding encouragement to the artificer and the labourer . . . we want people, we want sober and diligent tradesmen."

In Harrisburg, in 1828, a smith advertised:

> William Carson, Tin-Plate Worker, respectfully informs the public that he carries on the above business, in all its various branches, in Second Street next door to Dr. Luthers, in the shop formerly owned by John Martin, where he has on hand japan'd ware, steamers and boilers, Rumpet's Roasters and new improved ovens.

Papers from Thompson's General Store at Thompsontown, Pennsylvania, mention ware bought from two smiths, Jacob Boas and William Martin, the latter from Harrisburg. In 1801, Boas sold Thompson buckets in two sizes, watering pots, coffeepots, milk strainers, and quart measures. The ware traveled to Thompsontown by a boat operated by a gentleman named Holman. Thompson's order arrived at his store accompanied by this note:

OTHER PENNSYLVANIA TINMEN

(Left) Hooked-spout coffeepot. Courtesy of Gina Martin, Wapping, Connecticut. (Right) Coffeepot in red with bottom edge darkened by heat. Courtesy of the Philadelphia Museum of Art, Philadelphia, Pennsylvania.

Honored Friend:

By the bearor Holman I send you the ware after your Directions. But a few artickles I could not find the full number of. Holman was in a hurry so I sent you what I had. Hoping it will come safe to hand.

I am your Respected Friend
Jacob Boas

PRICES

Another invoice shows items bought by Thompson from John Martin in 1820:

½ dozen large buckets	$4.20
½ dozen small buckets	3.00
½ dozen 3 quart coffeepots	1.80

3 three quart coffee boilers	.90
1 dozen water ladles	1.50
6 dozen tin cups	4.20
1 dozen patty pans	1.20
½ dozen hand basins	1.80
½ dozen quart measures	.60

Prices charged by smiths in different localities varied. The ledger of Thomas Haywood of Woodstock, Connecticut, covering a period from 1806 to 1820, also reveals retail prices:

Tumbler	$ .12
Roasting oven	5.00
Milk pans	.37
Pails	1.00
Coffeepots	1.00
Lanterns	1.00 and 2.00
Pr. of candlesticks	.57

In Georgetown, District of Columbia, William Thomson was a tinsmith. In 1806, he charged Edward Smith $1.64 for: a watering pot, teakettle, colander, bread basket, snuffer tray, and pint cup. During December, 1806, Thomson sold Thomas Jefferson a scoop and two coffeepots. Francis Scott Key bought a ladle, a piece of tinware for his church, and asked the smith to mend a fender chafing dish and a teakettle.

A novel tinshop was reported by traveler Timothy Flint in *Recollections of the Last Ten Years*, published in Boston in 1826. With his family he went from Connecticut to the Mississippi and down the river. He wrote:

> While I was at New Madrid (in Missouri), a large tinner's manufactory floated there in a boat. In it all the different articles of tinware were manufactured and sold by wholesale and by retail. There were three large apartments, where the different branches of the art were carried on

A FLOATING TIN SHOP

in this floating manufactory. When they had mended all the tin, and vended all that they could sell in one place, they floated on to another.

The idea of the floating store had been used before in this country. General stores floated along the New England coast, the Erie Canal, and the Susquehanna River, although this floating tin shop is the only one of which I have heard.

DECORATION

Among the fine collections of tinware in Pennsylvania two important types of decoration are found: punched or wriggled decoration resulting from the use of chisels or other sharp instruments directly on bare metal, and the kind of painted ornamentation that has become familiar in the discussions of decoration found in other states. The truly distinctive ware of Pennsylvania, that which her smiths pierced and punched, includes unique and ingenious pieces.

Piercing and punching were sometimes utilitarian and sometimes for decorative effect. Designs were made by the use of punches and chisels of various shapes and sizes. A boss, or raised spot in the metal, was made with a blunt punch, hence the term "punched ware"; a slit through the metal resulted from a blow of a chisel, hence the term "pierced ware." The fanciest of these wares were usually the punched coffeepots. Their component parts were ornamented before they were soldered together, the work done with what would become the inside of the piece uppermost, so that after punching and soldering together, the bosses formed a bas-relief on the outside.

Cheese molds and foot warmers were pierced. A food safe, made of wooden frame with pierced tin panels, has become a coveted piece of antique furniture. Sometimes these cupboards sat

(Top) Wriggled coffeepot with finely executed design showing dove with olive branch. Note reinforced handle. (Bottom) Other side has warlike eagle. Courtesy of H. F. Du Pont Winterthur Museum, Winterthur, Delaware.

on the floor, occasionally they were suspended from ceiling beams. These were used, often in the pantry, to store meat or baked goods.

Wriggling is accomplished by incising a design on the metal with sharp blows upon a fine chisel, moving the chisel minutely with each blow. The result is somewhat like etching. Two particularly expert examples of this decoration may be found on a coffeepot initialed "J. M." which is displayed at the Hershey Estates Museum at Hershey, Pennsylvania Birds executed in detail are the motifs on both of these pieces. Another fine wriggled coffeepot may be seen in the Henry Francis DuPont Winterthur Museum. This appears to represent War and Peace, with an eagle holding a serpent in his beak on one side and a dove holding an olive branch on the other.

These designs imposed directly upon the metal are sometimes realistic, sometimes stylized, sometimes crude. Birds, tulips, and geometric designs closely related to fraktur, "Pennsylvania Dutch" embroidery and coverlets, and the ornamentation on Pennsylvania chests, make up the largest percentage of the designs used. Initials and dates appear once in a while, worked into the pattern.

The names of a few men who practiced this art are known. In the middle of the nineteenth century they signed their work with names stamped into the metal, usually on the handles of coffeepots. D. Gilbert of Pottstown, John and P. Shade of Berks County, M. Uebele and J. Ketterer followed this practice. Diligent research has uncovered no ledger or documents of any sort to augment the little known of these particular tinmen.

In Pennsylvania a comparatively large amount of crystallized tinware has been found. Crystal-

Rare punched box with delicate design. Top has early favorite, weeping willow tree. Courtesy of H. F. Du Pont Winterthur Museum, Winterthur, Delaware.

lization is caused by the use of acid on metal—here is a set of instructions:

> Take sheet-metal, the best and thickest covered with metal you can get, clean it well with whiting and water till the face is well polished. Warm it or lay it on a hot plate and with a sponge or brush wet it well with strong spirits of salts. You will soon see it shoot into beautiful patterns; as soon as this happens plunge it into cold spring water. You may then varnish it with any color you please or leave it in its natural state and varnish it with clear varnish.
>
> from *The Cabinet-Makers Guide*

The result is a sparkling surface shot with highlights. Crystallization is usually used on the floor of a coffin lid tray, or on a bread or apple tray, in combination with a border pattern painted on a band. Little ware of this sort is found outside of Pennsylvania.

Painted patterns on tinware originating in Pennsylvania, the work of native Pennsylvanians, is hard to identify as such. Contrary to the situation with pierced and punched ware, there seems to be little relationship between painted ware found in the Dutch State and the decoration on furniture, boxes, and fraktur indigenous to Pennsylvania and central European countries. Although tulips are found on Pennsylvania-painted tinware, this is true of ware decorated in New York and in Maine. I do not believe that the painted patterns incorporating bird and heart motifs are typical of Pennsylvania painting. Ann Butler of East Greenville, New York, used a heart as the trademark which sometimes framed her initials and Augustus Filley sent back to Con-

Unusual candle shade; punched and pierced. Courtesy of Julian Milliman.

Wriggled coffeepot with conical lid and detailed bird design. Courtesy of Hershey Museum, Hershey, Pennsylvania.

Hooked-spout punched coffeepot with delicate but primitive pattern. Collection of the author.

necticut for trays "with birds on them if you please" to sell in New York State.

It has been suggested that some of Pennsylvania's country tinware was imported from Britain. This, of course, may be true. I doubt that it is, though, for the type of design which we relegate to country tinware is unfamiliar on tin or ironware which is identifiable as British. A more formal type of painting, sometimes designated by decorators as "Chippendale painting," is found in Pennsylvania as well as in other states. This can sometimes be positively identified as British by an export stamp on the bottom.

Many of the painted pieces found in Pennsylvania appear to be the work of Filley shops.

Harvey Filley, who managed a shop in Philadelphia from the first of the 1820s until at least 1850, was himself a decorator as well as a tinsmith. Records show that over a period of years Harvey employed japanners and decorators imported from Berlin, Connecticut. This is one explanation for the fact that one finds decoration on some tinware discovered in Pennsylvania very like decoration found in Connecticut. It seems only logical, however, that some of Harvey's apprentice painters should have been native Pennsylvanians who might have adapted conventional patterns to appeal to the "Gay Dutch." An attempt to provide such appeal may explain some of the especially gaudy patterns and the frequent use of red as a background paint.

Perhaps Jacob Eicholtz, mentioned earlier as a tinsmith-turned-artist, sometimes ornamented

Deed box with drawer-pull handle, bold white flowers. Courtesy of Sara Fuller, Bryn Mawr, Pennsylvania.

his tinware. There is little record of this supposition except a reference by a Mr. Russel who wrote an article "Eichold, the painter" published in *Portfolio* in April, 1811:

> Eichold entered into the manufactory of tin. The pots and kettles which he then offered for sale, were generally ornamented with some fanciful painting of his own. But the celebrity such trifling daubs acquired among the phlegmatic Dutch was not sufficient to satisfy a man like Eichold.

As early as 1794 a Philadelphia directory listed "Cotton and Careless, Japanners," and in the nineteenth century many advertisements like the ones which follow were published. (Note that the types of decoration referred to below are gold-leaf work and stenciling.)

> Japanning establishment – Dan'l Dick & Co. Successors to Thomas Blackmore have moved from 239 S. 5th Street to Wheeler's Court and St. James Street. All orders in Japanning, Fancy and Ornamental, got up in the best style – sign writing, Gilding, Bronzing, Grocer's Canisters, & all kinds of Tinmen's Work done in a superior manner at short notice.

> James C. Cravens Manufactory – 4 North 7th St. A general assortment of Fancy, Bright Work, all of the best quality, Japanned Ware of all sorts with bronze, extra gilt japanning, all of the best quality which will be sold wholesale and retail at the most reduced rates. Shopkeepers and persons starting housekeeping are requested to call.

Cornelius Weygandt's *The Dutch Country* is a charming book, and in it, Mr. Weygandt recalls having known of a tinware painter, the grandfather of his friend Solomon. First he says, "For forty years I have known the neighborhood . . . folks from as far away as Lebanon in one direction and Honey Brook in the other have spoken of painted toleware as New Holland tin." (New Holland is just east of Bareville and northeast of Lancaster.) Mr. Weygandt reminisces:

I think of such a little shop as that of the grandfather of my friend Solomon, up on the Lehigh Mountain, the only shop where tin was painted of which I have firsthand information. This shop takes us back to 1830, more than a hundred years ago, when, in that remote locality, stencils were just coming into use but were not yet considered best form in tray painting. Solomon thinks work just as good as that of old pre-stencilling days could be done now if we could get the old paints and the old heavy tin. The tinker, as the tinsmith was often called in Pennsylvania, would bring his carefully-made coffee-pots and nutmeg graters and needle cases, and sugar bowls and egg servers and little safes, his trays and measures and spice boxes to Solomon's grandfather, and leave them with him to paint leisurely and with studied care with traditional decorations and colors.

Leaves from
the Journals of
a Smith,
a Peddler, and
a Tinker

*I*T SEEMS like pure luck, for in this research there has been a heaping portion of coincidence. For instance: first, the curator of the New York State Historical Association showed me a tray inscribed "Mercy North"; soon afterward a librarian from Yale told me that the university owned ledgers from the tool-making North family of Berlin, Connecticut; and then Dr. Charles Montgomery, Director of the Henry Francis Dupont Winterthur Museum, offered his personal collection of business correspondence between members of the same family. This information has been passed on to you in previous chapters.

Early in this game of "seek-and-seek," the diary of a tin peddler, William Holbrook, was brought to my attention at the New York State Library. Shortly after that, a correspondent from the Baker Library at Harvard University notified me that their archives held notebooks and ledgers recording the accounts of master tinsmith Morillo Noyes who was Holbrook's employer.

STATE OF VERMONT, SS.

$15

BE IT KNOWN, THAT LICENSE IS HEREBY GRANTED TO

Vilas Hayes — of *Brulington* in the county of *Chittenden* and State of *Vermont* to be a PEDLAR within this State for one year from the date hereof, for the purpose of pedling goods, wares and merchandise, (except jewelry,) of the growth and manufacture of the United States, and he has paid therefor the sum of *Fifteen* dollars.

Given under my hand, this *28* day of *March* A. D. 184*5*.

John Spaulding State Treasurer.

E. A. Stansbury Clerk of
County.

Peddling license. Courtesy of Baker Library, Harvard University, Cambridge, Massachusetts.

MORILLO NOYES

Holbrook's diary and the memorandum books of Noyes, director of widespread peddling operations out of Burlington, Vermont, picture tinmen and peddlers and their transactions in New York, Vermont, Massachusetts, and Canada in the mid-eighteen hundreds. Noyes was a hardworking, shrewd Yankee and a demanding master, ready to turn an honest dollar any way he could. He was part-owner of the Winooski Cotton Mills and of the *Burlington Democrat*. An ardent Democrat himself, he was positive that Greeley would defeat Grant in the presidential election.

The master smith ran his wholesale business from before 1850 until 1875, allowing himself at one time a thousand dollars a year salary. He bought and sold from Boston to New York to Canada and points in between. In 1859, Noyes hired twelve peddlers to cover his routes. At that time the business owned eighteen horses. It cost Noyes twenty-five dollars a day to lodge his tinmen and thirty-six dollars for his peddlers.

By 1861, he had twenty-five peddlers on the road, and some of them evidently owned their own outfits, for in inventory Noyes listed only seven wagons valued at $525, four pairs of "sledding sleighs" at $80, and a single sleigh worth $15.

In 1862, Noyes mentioned visiting another master smith because he hoped to rent some carts. The smith was Crampten of Rutland who owned

English wax-faced peddler doll. Courtesy of The New-York Historical Society, New York City.

sixteen peddling outfits and had only six hired peddlers out. Shedd and Walker were also mentioned as contemporary smiths. According to Noyes, "They have twenty-four peddlers. This is about as many as they want to send out. Take too much credit to run more this year." An earlier entry had noted, "Money is horable tight."

In 1863, Noyes had nine tinsmiths in his shop and boasted a "good assortment of tin" on hand. One smith could keep several peddlers supplied. Noyes complained, though, that the smiths had only a few pans ahead, never too many. In October of the next year, the master smith had on hand twenty-five hundred dollars' worth of tinware and eighteen hundred dollars' worth of other stock which included linen thread, spools, pins, combs, needles, suspenders, soap, hooks, eyes, and matches. This variety shows the change which had taken place in the peddlers' stock

Deed box. Courtesy of the late Violet M. Scott, Uxbridge, Massachusetts.

Coffeepot. Courtesy of Florence Wright, Penn Yan, New York.

WILLIAM HOLBROOK

after 1850. Sundries had become popular with peddlers, perhaps because the average profit on small items was 150 per cent. Although Noyes paid 7 per cent to borrow cash, the mark-up on tin was 40 per cent, also a high profit when compared with other manufactures.

From his diary, complete for the year 1854, one finds that peddler Holbrook's duties were multiple. He sold tinware directly to stores and took orders for future deliveries, bought all sorts of barter accumulated by country merchants and purchased such items as furs directly from the men who trapped them. When he traveled, considerable time was spent sacking barter for shipment back to Burlington by the most appropriate means of transportation available, usually train or boat. Holbrook interviewed others who were interested in peddling for Noyes, acted as collection agent, and wrote a daily report back to Burlington. On one tour Holbrook was away from Burlington for four and a half months, driving his horse and wagon twenty-five hundred miles. Personal expenses amounted to $236 in cash; $1,300 was expended for bartered produce which he purchased from country storekeepers; $500 was collected in back bills; and $600 in "foreign money" was sent back to Burlington. Over two hundred sacks for shipping barter were sent to Holbrook at different points along his route and Mr. Noyes sent him seventy-nine letters of instruction. At home after his trip he noted that he still had "a multiplicity of reports" to make.

Holbrook was a diligent, serious young man. He was unmarried in 1854 when he was thirty-five, although he mourned the death in 1850 of "beloved Susan, Companion." Whether she was fiancée or wife, I could not discover. With parents dead and one brother en route to Wisconsin to live, the peddler's life was a lonely one. He was far from robust and the life he led was a rigorous one—on the road winter as well as summer. "I feel more like lying still than circulating," he wrote. In January he noted, "Strong south wind, but cold. I feel nearly used up, walking yesterday and getting chilled." (His horse had fallen part way through the ice and damaged the tin cart so that it had been necessary for the peddler to travel for miles on foot.) Another time he wrote, "Caught in a thunder shower. Wet as a rat." Again, "Plank road, else I should have had a hard time, as the roads are horrible."

Holbrook was fond of good food, although he kept his purse strings tight and disliked paying more than he thought a meal was worth. He lamented the fact that so many of his fellows enjoyed "liquor sauce," and whenever possible he sought out "dry" hotels. An entry in the diary reports, "Arrived at Captain Benedict's, Crown Point, New York, a little before Sunset, and glad to find a Temperance House for the Sabbath, a very good house, so-called." Holbrook identified one hotel at Chateaugay as "Martin's Drunken Hole." At Champlain, however, he found attractive accommodations, dined in luxury, and paid 62½ cents for dinner and housekeeping. At Waterloo he was "drove out of bed by an army of bedbugs." Another time, in Fort Covington, "Oh the musketoes—enough to kill body and soul. No sleep nor rest on the bed, then under it, then on the piazzo." Once he complained that

Box with symmetrical pattern. Example of green leaves so darkened they are almost invisible. Courtesy of James Stevens, Greenville, New York.

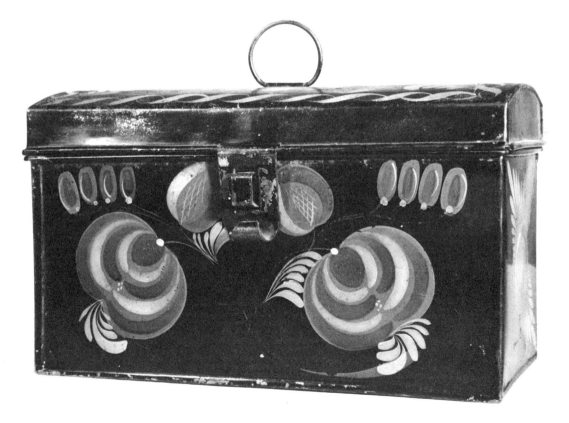

there was "dancing at the sound of the violin an hour or two past midnight" making sleep impossible. Later, "Plague take a Snorer!"

The peddler regretted the observance on July 4 of a celebration which kept tradesmen from their stores so that he "could do nothing." Ordinarily he traveled and called on customers all day. At night he sacked barter, arranged for its shipping, and wrote reports to Morillo Noyes.

On January 3, 1854, he was in Berkshire Center, Vermont, where he sold a Mr. Carpenter tinware worth $192.23. He received in part payment thirty-four dozen pairs of socks valued at $102. He was at this time en route home to settle up for his tour. After the settlement he rejoiced, "Came out Even, for Once!"

Immediately, though, he started out again, this time through Vergennes, Middlebury, Brandon, and Rutland, Vermont. Along the way he made a deal with a farmer for ninety pelts at 63 cents a pelt and later decided that he had "got shaved." In Rutland he called at the shop of Crampten and Johnson where he found that the latter had died of inflammatory rheumatism. In West Rutland he attended the funeral of William Brown of Clarendon Springs who had died "Thursday last, in a fit outdoors, face in the Mud, aged 29. Wife and one child—highly respected—buried in full dress, natural as life."

From the Rutlands he went to Fair Haven, then south to Troy, New York, to call on Mrs. Edge, a mattress manufacturer whom he wished to supply with bartered hair. He visited Albany, New York, then turned north, going through Castleton and the Poultneys in Vermont and the Granvilles in New York. He mentioned that his horse was loaded heavily with from ten to twelve hundred pounds. Salem, New York, was next

Square candlestick with raised bottom. The simple design is quite rare. Collection of the author.

on his route; there he drove through a strong wind and "almost perished with the cold." Holbrook did business in Shushan and White Creek, New York, and visited the Bennington, Vermont, potteries at which he marveled. According to the peddler the pottery was "truly worth examining—truly a great Curiosity, to behold the genius of Experienced Workmen in forming so readily their different shaped Wares with a Lump of Clay prepared in a nice consistency for Work."

From Bennington, Holbrook went to Shaftsbury, Factory Point, Danbury, and North Wallingford where he traded a little with a tinman named Stafford, "a young man of respectable appearance." Rutland was again his next stop so that he might pick up sacks shipped there by train for him. He stayed at the Franklin House for the night and for breakfast; charged $1.25, he declared, "Perfect Robbery! Rutland is the hardest place all-in-all that I can find, seems to be the understanding of Every man to Shave every Customer he has."

On his thirty-fifth birthday, Holbrook started on a trip to Ticonderoga, Crown Point, and Westport, New York. At Richards Hotel in Westport he exhibited samples of goods and traded with F. H. Page. Again he had reached the end of a tour and he headed home, crossing over to Charlotte, Vermont, on the ice of Lake Champlain. It took a day or two to examine barter, check prices, and settle accounts with Noyes.

Excerpts from the diary fill in some of the details of his trips (starting out in northern New York State):

March 16 – Very pleasant day. Thaws fast – I tried to do some business but after looking about for a few hours conclude that I can not find much to do advantageously – a little before noon went (rowboat) to Prescott, and run over this Canadian village – nothing very attractive here that I could behold. Saw Claudius Mills here. He is painting Steam Boats.

April 9 – Went to Trout River, Canada line, called on merchants. Five miles *bad* road. Thence to Constable, and on to Malone. No trade but deep mud and stony roads.

April 15 – Rec'd order for Tinware for nearly fifty dollars, thence to Canton Village and Bot and Sacked 1,289 lbs. at three and a half delivered at Madrid Depot. 71 lbs. copper @ .22 and 29½ lbs. brass @ .15.

May 24 – Chateaugay – I remained with "Mine Host" during yesterday. Well pleased with the arrangement Excepting the liquor traffic (moderately used only) in this respect I can not help the Matter, though gladly would I see it *discontinued* and *discountenanced* throughout the land.

June 2 – Westport – Circus here. Levi J. North's – bad luck coming – turned over one of two wagons – one span of horses down an embankment. Broke one of their legs, killed them. Put up at private house in Essex, N.Y. N. Clemons having discontinued tavern.

June 13 – Remained in bed undergoing perspiring operations over the region of the liver – hot woolen cloths saturated – soaked in a solution of Smart Weed and Hops, applied hot and changed every fifteen minutes. Pd. doctor Sprague $3.48 in full.

June 28 – Called on A. Sawyer, Tanner. Think I shall effect a trade. Bot the largest amount of stub hair I ever Bot. 336 pounds.

August 29 – Met George Brewster on his way to Essex with a drove of cattle.

September 23 – Have not done a cent's worth of business today! Too bad to work so hard over hills and rocks for nothing – Can't help it. So goes the world.

JAMES GUILD, PEDDLER AND TINKER

Like William Holbrook, James Guild kept a diary. From this we discover that not all peddlers were as persistent as Holbrook when business was bad. Guild lived in Halifax, Vermont, and, when he turned twenty-one in 1818, he decided to invest in a peddler's kit: "No one knows the feelings of my heart when parting with my all for a trunk of goods and losing my caricter if I had any by being a pedlar." He complained that it was difficult for a farm boy to "put on a pedlar's face."

Guild headed west on foot through New York State but lacked confidence in his ability as a salesman. During one three-day period he sold thirty cents' worth of goods and gave away more than he sold. Having covered a considerable distance only to discover that he was a complete failure financially, Guild abandoned peddling to take up tinkering.

All tinsmiths were tinkers: they mended worn tinware. One tinman sounds like a plastic surgeon—his ledger itemizes "ear on pail—$.06," "nose on watering pot—$.18." The true tinker, however, was an itinerant who mended pots and pans and made small custom orders. He was frequently known by his "theme song" or chant which became familiar in the villages as well as along country lanes.

> Tinker pots, tinker pots,
> Bring out your pans.

or

> Has anyone got any boilers to mend?
> If they have
> Here's the man who can do it,
> Can do it,
> Can do it.

In the country the tinker was apt to travel on horseback, saddlebags filled with solder, old lead, and a soldering iron, a spoon mold, a clock dial mold, and bits of tinplate—ready to tin the bottom of a teakettle, mend a hole in a pan, or cast a spoon. He made cookie cutters to order to fit the fancy of the housewife. By reputation he was as tough as the Georgia tinker who was said to have melted his solder over an open flame and stirred it with his finger.

The tinker, though, was at the bottom of the social barrel. When Mary Ball Washington wrote to her brother that teen-age George might go to sea, Joseph Ball hurried to show his distaste for the navy by sarcastically recommending tinkering as a preferable alternative.

> Stratford Bow, London
> 19th May, 1747
>
> Dear Sister:
>
> I understand that you are advised and have some thoughts of putting your son George to sea. I think he had better be put prentice to a tinker, for a common sailor before the mast has by no means the common liberty of the subject; for they will press him for a ship where he has fifty shillings a month and make him take twenty, and cut and slash him like a Negro, or rather like a dog.
>
> Your loving brother,
> Joseph Ball

P. T. Barnum wrote, "The idea that a shoemaker or a tinker can not be a gentleman is simply ridiculous," but Barnum seems to have been fighting a losing battle; James Guild noted:

> I told them that I was going to get an old leathern apron and some spoon molds and go around a-tinkering. As I had got to be mean, I would be mean. I told the folks of all my misfortunes. They seemed to feel a tenderness for me but I told them that I had concluded to be a poor man the rest of my days and I was going

Teapot. Courtesy of The
Henry Ford Museum,
Dearborn, Michigan.

to pursue some employment that would set me
below the common class of people. . . . The
gentleman replied, "If that is all you want I can
help you get a leather apron and I guess my
neighbor Thompson has got a pair of spoon
molds and you can buy them." I presume that I
told him that if I could not be in a situation to
live in good society I wanted to appear so mean
that no one would take notice of me. He laughed
at my nonsense but I told him to fetch my leather
apron and he got it and I put in on and went
to make a bargain for the spoon molds. Now
there was laughing enough. My clothes were become poor, my hat rather mean, and I combed
my hair down over my eyes and got me a little
soldering iron and prepared for a tinker. Now I
cared not for my looks or my reputation and I
had deformed myself so that if I were to meet
my mother on the road I believed she would not
know me. Now I went on and come to a house
and inquired whether or not they wanted any
spoons run or any tinkering done. The reply was,
"Can you run old plates into spoons?"

"Oh, yes, Mam, I can mend your arson ware
for I have got some cement for that purpose."

Document box with quizzical
owl. Courtesy of the
Philadelphia Museum of Art,
Philadelphia, Pennsylvania.

So the old woman fetched on some pewter plates
and I went to mending them up. Oh how my
friends would have laughed could they have seen
me in this situation. There was one thing on my
side – that is they could not laugh me to scorn
for I was below that. Then, however, I went to
running spoons and I run twelve spoons and had
thirty cents for doing it . . .

In this style I was spending my time which I
thought was a meaner calling than I deserved,
for I felt at this time as mean as my employ.

In contrast to Guild was the happy tinker
whose story is recounted in this ballad which
I first heard when it was sung by Frank Warner:

I am a jolly tinker,
That goes from town to town.
I will mend your pots and kittles
If you'll only bring them 'round.

Chorus:
Tura laddy, tura laddy,
Tura laddy, hi row.

I know how to solder,
And I can mend a pot,

I can also stop a hole
So it will not leak a drop.

I can mend umbrellas,
And I can tinker clocks,
The housewives are all smiles
When they see the tinker stop.

A tinker never marries,
Has a girl in every town,
And they shower me with kisses
As they bring their kittles down.

They feast me and regale me,
With choicest meat and wine,
And whatever house I stop at
I can always sup and dine.

So many wait my coming
For I have many friends.
I have never stored much gold
Yet I have a lot to spend.

My life is wild and free,
I do not seek renown.
I'm just a jolly tinker
With a girl in every town.

Peddler
Folklore

*T*HERE ARE all sorts of stories about tin peddlers in the places these gentlemen of the road used to frequent. Some of the stories are true; some are half-true; and some haven't an ounce of truth in them.

> "I'll take old copper, old brass, old iron and pewter, old rags, anything except cash and old maids."
>
> Peddler's call

One acquaintance of mine reminisced recently to say that a peddler was responsible for a household saying in his family. The tin peddler who regularly traveled a route past the friend's home had a hound that was always hungry; so, around the Patterson farm in West Fort Ann, New York, if anyone was really famished, he was "hungry as a peddler's hound."

In *The Life of P. T. Barnum* written by Himself (according to the title page) the author tells of working in a Connecticut country store. Some peddler had been very persuasive and a too-large supply of tinware on the shelves was growing old and dull. Barnum wanted to buy new ware but could not until the old stock had been dispersed. So, he organized a lottery, sold chances to all the customers, drew lots, and paid off—chiefly in old tinware. Barnum mentions that not all of the winners were pleased, but the store's shelves were cleaned off, and he was able to order bright ware to tempt local housewives.

Occasionally tinmen, like all tradesmen, had trouble convincing customers that they should pay up their accounts. Tinman Russell M. Gallup of Unadilla, New York, had this verse published in the *Freeman's Journal* of Cooperstown on July 18, 1831, "A New Plan to Cheat Lawyers, Starve Justices and Cause Constables to Beg for Work":

Pay Your Debts When Due or Before

The tinman finds that if he waits,
A few more years, 'twill be too late
For to collect a few demands
Which he now has on his hands.

Therefore he hopes without delay,
Those who do owe will stop and pay,
For in that way they will save costs
And if they don't it will be lost.

I hope this call will not be neglected,
Nor another call expected,
For then a louder call they'll hear,
Which unto them will prove quite dear.

The Connecticut peddler who met the Honorable Elisha Potter in the middle of a narrow causeway was obstinate. There was no room for cart and buggy to pass and neither driver was about to back up. The Squire unbuttoned his waistcoat, took out his newspaper and settled back to read in a leisurely fashion. After some time, just as the Squire thought he had out-sat the peddler, the latter called out, "I say, Squire, when you've committed that paper to heart, please allow me chance to peruse it." The Honorable Mr. Potter grumbled, and retreated, allowing the peddler to cross first.

Upon rare occasions, though, it was the peddler who was bested by one of his countrymen,

Small bun tray signed on floor, "Maria Osman." Courtesy of H. F. Du Pont Winterthur Museum, Winterthur, Delaware.

a feat to retell beside the cracker barrel. Ben Barrett of Luzerne, New York, was a notorious practical joker, always primed and cocked for a prank. He saw a peddler about to cross a bridge on foot and bet him a small sum that he could carry his heavy basket of tinware across faster than the peddler could run without it. The race began; it progressed uneventfully until both were about at the middle. Then Ben fell deliberately, crushing the ware in the basket. He paid his bet willingly and strutted off laughing as the peddler mournfully examined his damaged utensils.

"Doc" Carrington, a country merchant from near Danbury, Connecticut, figured he, too, had been bested once too often by a smart peddler, and vowed to get even. An unsuspecting tin and sundry peddler visited Doc and offered to sell to the merchant at wholesale prices and take unsalable goods off his hands for the retail price. The storekeeper chose a gross of whetstones at three dollars a dozen. The peddler reckoned the bill at thirty-six dollars and asked what the storekeeper had that he couldn't sell.

"Whetstones, at 50 cents apiece," said Doc.

"Took in, by hookey!" said the peddler. By

mutual agreement he gave the storekeeper a dollar in cash, took back his whetstones and hurried on his way.

The Reverend Timothy Dwight would have enjoyed Doc's trick on the peddler. He made no bones about his feeling toward the whole fraternity:

> Many of the men today employed in this business part at an early age with both honesty and principle. Their sobriety is exchanged for cunning, their hearty honesty for imposition, and their decent behavior for coarse impudence.

There were just enough peddlers who felt the need to live up to their "wooden nutmeg" reputation to keep peddler history lively. Oscar Fillmore of Ballston Spa, New York, who worked for Tracy Brothers, was one of these. Oscar chuckled as he told about the time when he stopped in a certain farmyard in hopes of making a sale. He was met by a housewife who confided that her husband was away and asked the peddler's name. She hurried to explain that the farmer had warned her not to trade with a peddler named Fillmore because he would "steal her blind." Oscar promptly adopted a new name and inveigled the woman into buying several pieces of tinware. Driving out of the yard he met the husband who called, "Hallo there, Fillmore." Oscar touched his horse with the whip and galloped off. When asked why he hurried the peddler confessed, "The old codger'd told her I'd steal her blind, so I did!"

Another peddler got his own way. He was riding on a stagecoach which stopped for dinner at an inn. The peddler knew that the innkeeper had connived with the stage driver to summon his passengers before they could eat the food they had bought. When the driver's shout interrupted the travelers' meal, the peddler nonchalantly continued to eat and allowed the stagecoach to leave without him. After his leisurely main course he ordered a custard for dessert. Shouting for the landlord, the diner demanded a spoon, asking what had become of all those which had been on the table and suggesting that he knew which angry diner had taken them in spite.

A stable boy was dispatched in hot pursuit of the stage and soon driver and irate passengers returned. As the peddler, who had meantime finished his custard, climbed aboard, the innkeeper demanded that he point out the man who had taken the spoons.

"Sure," said the peddler, "I took them myself. You will find every one of them in the big coffeepot on the table. C'mon driver, let's be going."

These itinerants *were* shrewd, and many a famous fortune, such as that of the Gimbel family, grew from a peddler's nest egg. Peddlers who were really dishonest, though, were probably scarce. "Honest" Wilson of Barre, Vermont, traveled the length and breadth of his state for fifteen years, true to his nickname.

Peddler Ted was a handsome, virile young man. In peddling, romancing, and square-dancing, he excelled. His voice was a familiar one in the Adirondacks where he sang out his ware as he approached each house, itemizing the articles he carried so that eager housewives waited for him, egg money jingling in their apron pockets. Successful in business and eventually in love, Ted astounded the solemn guests at his wedding. When the preacher directed Ted and the bride to join hands, the groom forgot where he was and shouted with a caper, "Join hands and circle to the left. . . ."

Coffeepot signed on bottom, "William Eno, Simsbury, Conn." Courtesy of the Philadelphia Museum of Art, Philadelphia, Pennsylvania.

Another romantic peddler was Yankee Robinson. Yankee had "graduated" from a Shaker colony, and he, too, hankered for a wedding. He advertised in the newspaper to find a bride. An eager prospect was carefully picked from those who answerd his proposal, and the peddler planned the nuptials. When the bride arrived in town, friends of the groom met her and conveyed her to the church where she found her prospective mate at the church door, ready to sell tickets to the much-publicized mail-order wedding. Only protests from indignant church elders prevented the groom from collecting an admission fee.

Ne'er-do-well Sam Stewart, who lived in Poverty Hollow near Catskill, New York, was the victim of a near-fatal accident. The owner of a horse and wagon, Sam, when ambitious, peddled tin. One afternoon he snoozed as his horse pulled his loaded cart. Without a guide, the nag wandered off the road to browse and, turning down a sharp incline, overturned cart and driver. Sam suffered a severe head laceration and, when discovered, was taken to a nearby physician. Although the doctor found trepanning necessary, the patient recovered. Sam was full of gratitude for the surgeon; he delighted in exhibiting his scar, vowing to awestruck observers that he'd have died if Doc hadn't "japanned" him!

In an old rhyme, Hugh Peters describes how a tin peddler turned the tables on a landlord.

> There is a famous Yankee-land,
> A class of men ycleped [called] tin-pedlars,
> A shrewd, sarcastic band
> Of busy meddlers;
> They scour the country through and through,
> Vending their wares, tin pots, tin pans,
> Tin ovens, dippers, wash bowls, cans,
> Tin whistles, kettles, or to boil or stew,
> Tin dullenders, tin nutmeg graters,
> Tin warming pans for fish and 'taters!
> In short,
> If you will look within
> His cart,
> And gaze upon the tin
> Which glitters there,
> So bright and fair,
> There is no danger in defying
> You to go off without buying.
>
> One of these cunning, keen-eyed gentry
> Stopped at a tavern in the country
> Just before night,
> And called for bitters—for himself, of course,
> And fodder, for his horse:
> This done, our worthy wight
> Informed his landlord that his purse was low,
> "Quite empty, I assure you, Sir, and so
> I wish you'd take your pay
> In something in my way."

Now Boniface supposed himself a wag—
And when he saw that he was sucked,
Was not dispirited, but plucked
Up courage and his trousers, too,
Quoth he t' himself, I am not apt to brag,
'Tis true,
But I can stick a feather in my cap
By making fun of this same Yankee chap.
"Well, my good friend,
That we may end this
Troublesome affair,
I'll take my pay in ware,
Provided that you've got what suits my inclina-
   tion."
"No doubt of that," the pedlar cried,
Sans hesitation:
"Well, bring us a pair of good tin boots!"
"Tin boots?" Our Jonathan espied
His landlord's spindle shanks,
And giving his good Genius thanks
For the suggestion,
Ran out, returned, and then—"By goles!
Yes, here's a pair of candlemolds!
They'll fit you without question!"

The tales of murdered peddlers are numerous. Perhaps even now our back-country roads are manned by legions of reluctant ghosts, their carts rolling along silently at last. Wheaton P. Webb, in "Pedlar's Protest," explains the high mortality rate among peddlers:

> Every New York State village is bursting with legends of murdered tin pedlars. If tin pedlars are scarce these days, it is because a favorite pastime of Yorkers a generation ago was murdering these romantic itinerants for their gold, and burying their bodies in abandoned wells or under the floors of deserted barns. Every pedlar was supposed to carry a quantity of gold coin securely fastened in a belt slung around his middle and must have meant a pretty penny for the man who could slash his throat.

One of my young friends likes to recount a tale his grandmother told him of a peddler ghost, or part of one. As a child the boy was warned repeatedly against going through a particular part of the woods below Lake George, New York, because a ghostly arm and hand had frequently been seen there almost concealed behind rocks, where years before a peddler had been murdered and his body hidden.

Mr. Holman J. Swinney, a marvelous yarn-spinner, told this story. He later wrote it down so that I might retell it here in his exact words:

Uncle George Wilcox lived in North Brookfield, New York, until he died in about 1950 at the age of nearly eighty. He told of driving through the woods with his grandfather, Aaron, a wagon-maker, in the days when he was a boy. They came to a place where the road split, one branch going over the hill, the newer, lower down. At the top of the hill lived Leev Johnson, an old, old man, the last of his tribe, in a house which had long since fallen down. Uncle George said the man lived in the cellar and kept his fire in a "cauldron kittle." The story went that the old man's family had murdered a tin peddler for his money and buried the man in a spot later passed over by the new road.

Uncle George's grandfather chose to drive over the hill on the old road. The old man with his long hair and queer old-fashioned hat stopped them at the top of the hill.

"Uncle Aaron," growled Leev, "why didn't you drive over the new road?"

"Because I didn't want to drive over the peddler's bones," said Aaron.

"God damn!" exploded the old man, and he tore off his hat. He threw it on the ground and stomped on it. When Aaron and Uncle George were off the hill, they could still see the old man against the sky, tearing his hair and jumping up and down.

Two or three days later Leev Johnson appeared at Aaron Wilcox's shop.

"Good morning, Aaron," he said with dignity.

"Mornin', Leev," said Aaron.

"You know them hickory trees you tried to buy off me three years ago, Aaron?"

"Yes, I do," said Aaron.

"Wouldn't sell them to you, would I? . . .
Well, now I'll sell them, and for three dollars
apiece, but on conditions."

"What are the conditions?" asked George's
grandfather warily.

"That you never mention them God-damned
peddler's bones again," roared the old man.

Canalers and lake sailors were reputedly tough
—among them fights were the rule, no holds
barred. Eyes were gouged, ears were chewed,
and sailors were handy with their knives. These
men on a holiday were wild. Such was the dis-
position of a crew bunking at an inn in Dresden
near Lake Champlain. The sailors drank until
midnight, then plotted to rob a tin peddler sleeping in an upstairs room. He was pulled from
his bed; when he resisted he was throttled and
dragged to the cellar where his body was stuffed
down a cistern.

Another York State inn played host to a kill-
ing. A certain tavern near Fishkill was a community center. On holidays there were turkey
and beef shoots, and the long straight road in
front of the ordinary was a drag strip where
farmers tested their favorite horses. When there
were horse races the loser often set up drinks
for all, to the delight of the landlord whose
avarice was notorious.

One evening as a storm arose, taproom regu-
lars scurried home. Unwittingly they left a lone
roomer, a peddler, at the mercy of the innkeeper.
Provided with this opportunity, he robbed and
did away with his guest. For two days the storm
continued and the local folks kept to their own
homes. The landlord was busy in the cellar and
the peddler never reappeared, alive. Years later
long-suspicious townfolk gathered tools and visited the then-abandoned hotel. As they reached
the cellar, they heard light footsteps overhead.

Upon investigation they found no one. When this happened a second time, the men dropped their tools and fled, giving up their search for the peddler's bones.

According to folk beliefs a person buried in unhallowed ground without a religious ceremony cannot remain at rest. This was the case with the two peddlers just described and both became "haunts." For years people around Dresden claimed that their ghost rose from his watery grave on the anniversary of his death and floated across the lake and back like a will-o'-the-wisp, uttering a sad, lingering cry. The ghost at Fishkill could be seen more often, wandering about the inn, usually in the cellar with a lantern, peering through the tiny windows. To my knowledge, the remains of these victims have never been disinterred and properly buried, so the restless spirits may still roam.

Red cream jug signed "Francis B. Richardson." Courtesy of H. F. Du Pont Winterthur Museum, Winterthur, Delaware.

Henry Backus, known as the Saugerties Bard, composed a ballad to tell the story of Hiram Williams, a peddler from New York City who was murdered in 1853:

Vouchsafe thine aid, ye wondrous nine,
To pen each sad and mournful line,
A tragic scene transpired of late,
A truth of which I will narrate.

On the Plank-Road in Greenville town,
A Jewish pedlar was shot down.
Ah, by a wretch called Warren Wood,
Who shot the pedlar in cold blood.

With murder rankling in his heart
From the Empire City did depart,
Armed with revolver, six-barreled, true,
With which he shot the pedling Jew.

To Albany his way he bent,
And money was his full intent.
Oh, had he pondered o'er the cost,
Two precious lives would not be lost.

Hiram Williams was the pedlar's name,
Who had obtained an honest fame.
He met with Wood, in Greenville town,
Where, sad to tell, he shot him down.

When first he shot, the pedlar cried,
Whate'er you want will be supplied.
His pocketbook to Wood he gave,
In hopes by this his life to save.

Again he shot! O cruel man!
What mortal can your feelings scan?
Infernal spirits astonished stood,
A while to gaze on Warren Wood.

Who did the pedlar's head then pound
As he lay bleeding on the ground,
Until he thought him truly dead,
And then the monster quickly fled.

Back to New York he sped his way,
To promenade with Ladies gay,
In Cherry Street they did him take: –
He now his pleasure must forsake.

Though filled with dread and guilty fear,
Before the pedlar must appear,

Thou art the man, the pedlar said
As he then raised his dying head.

I know that coat, the boots likewise –
A dying man will tell no lies,
To jail the Murderer then was sent,
His awful crimes there to lament.

In Christ the Saviour of mankind,
Repentance he will truly find;
Oh, soon he will suspended be,
To pay the law's just penalty.

A faithful jury did convict,
 The sheriff must the law inflict,
The penalty to justice due,
To all the guilty as to you.

No costly gems of diamonds bright,
Disarms the law or aids his flight,
Nor thousand tons of shining gold,
Yet, for a groat, Wood's life was sold.

No more, poor man, while here you stay,
The birds will chaunt their cheering lay,
Or friendly neighbors greet again
The wretch that hath the pedlar slain.

On January next, the twentieth day,
The Sheriff must the law obey,
 Upon the gallows him suspend,
 And thus poor Wood his life will end.

Let all a solemn warning take,
And every wicked way forsake,
For soon we all will usher'd be
Into a vast eternity.

Warren Wood was executed at the Greene County Jail, Catskill, New York, on June 20, 1854.

Near Crescent, New York, a ghostly peddler became a poltergeist to plague the tenants of the house where he had met death. The playful ghost delighted in standing at the foot of a bed to pull the covers from unwary sleepers. He opened and shut doors in quick succession all over the house, even after the doors had been nailed shut. After the peddler's skeleton was dis-

Ornate large Butler box mounted on tin ball feet. Brass lock, escutcheon, and handle. It has the signature of Ann Butler, the decorator, on the bottom. Courtesy of Mrs. Howard Adriance, Greenville, New York.

198

covered in an old spring and interred in a grave-yard, the house once more was peaceful.

How would you feel if there were blood-stains that wouldn't wash off the floor of your kitchen? Old Washington Fox, who lived near St. Johnsville, New York, was an ornery fellow who, in a rage, killed a peddler. The blood of the dying man soaked into the floor, and, although Mrs. "Wash" scrubbed on her hands and knees day after day, the stains always re-appeared as soon as the wide planks dried. Only a fire which consumed the whole house could destroy the stain.

Similar murder and ghost tales enliven our folk history. Circumstances often alter only slightly. The peddler who announced his approach by beating a tattoo on a small snare drum was slain, robbed, and buried in a berry patch on the outskirts of Cornwall, Connecticut. One can still, on special nights, hear the sound of his drum. Another phantom peddler drives his ancient horse down the road near Rhinecliff, New York, bouncing along with tin rattling as it swings from high racks. He drives as far as the place where robbers ambushed and killed him. From this point on down the road there is silence, until another black night when echoes of the cart and its jingling ware again resound.

There is another place where tinware rattles, though not because of murder. Natives say that whenever they ride over a certain spot in the road outside of Poestenkill, New York, they hear the clatter of tin on tin. Here in days when no crust of tar and gravel or concrete covered country lanes, an unsuspecting peddler drove into a "sinkhole." As folk watched in horror, the cart, tinware, horse, and driver sank in an instant. Bubbles in the oozing mire were soon all that remained. To this day the passing of a vehicle rattles the tinware, or so they say.

It has been easier to collect place names occasioned by peddlers and tinmen than to find the stories behind these names. Here is an exception, though. West of Charlton, New York, a road was named by a peddler. Often when he toured Schenectady County, he ended his day at twilight in this northern section of the county and usually he was invited to stay all right. The peddler, allergic to feathers, swore that every guest bed in every house on this road had a feather tick. He wheezed and sneezed and named the thoroughfare Featherbed Lane.

No Head Hill is on the road from Rupert, Vermont, to Salem, New York. Tragedy was enacted here, when a peddler was attacked and beheaded. On a subsequent evening an agitated traveler startled a farm family in a house down the hill by describing a headless man who had walked beside his horse, then crossed in front of him and run into the bushes. Search by lantern revealed no clues, and the blame was placed upon the ghost of the dead peddler, which, according to legend, has reappeared upon several occasions.

Horse Heaven Hill is another matter. This is in southern Vermont near Bellows Falls. A dilemma occurred when a heavily laden tin cart skidded out of control on a steep downgrade. The peddler realized that he could not save his cart and horse, so, like a ship's captain staying with his ship, he shouted to his horse, "Go to Heaven!" and plunged over the embankment.

Spook Bridge near Glenford and Pedlar's Bridge near New Rochelle, both in New York, were settings for peddler murders. Tin Peddlers' Path was along the Mohawk River near Rexford, New York. Tinsmith's Locks dammed the Delaware and Hudson Canal close to Honesdale, Pennsylvania. Tinker Hollow was near North Brookfield, New York; and there were two Tinker Hills that I know of—one named in the time of the Dutch, *Tinckner Hogen*, northwest of Amsterdam, New York, and the other three miles northeast of Canopus Hill in Putnam County, New York, the home of an English tinker named Cornelius Rick. Jerry Jingle Highway in Melrose, Massachusetts, was named after a tin peddler, I am told. Tinkertown once identified a section of Duxbury, Massachusetts. Tin Cup, Colorado, derived its name from the utensil used to measure gold dust. The story behind Peddler's Hill, Washingtonville, New York, is a mystery, but Spook Hollow, on the way to Milton, New York, was inspired by a peddler's ghost.

Today commercial metal workers are busy meeting the demands of food packagers and those in many other industries, and the small-town tinsmith has almost disappeared. The art of decorating tinware in the early manner has been revived because of such researcher-teachers as Esther Stevens Brazer, and many, today, enjoy practicing this art. No longer are the tin peddlers with us in person—the Fuller Brush men have taken their place. Yet, if we can believe what we hear, many old-time peddlers are still with us in spirit, driving down rural lanes, hiding in abandoned houses to bang doors and playfully snatch the bedcovers from any who challenge their rights.

Identification
and Care of
Old Tinware

*U*NTIL ANTIQUE TINWARE becomes as familiar as an old friend, it is difficult to separate it from new ware painted in the old manner. Sometimes even an owner does not know what he owns.

"Yes, I have several pieces of old tinware. Here's a lovely old tray." The *tray* was old, but the decoration was merely crude; it had been redone by an amateur.

"I'm especially proud of this antique piece. Great Aunt Abbie left it to me." Again this was an old tray with some original pattern—stenciling around the flange—but years after the tray had first been decorated, a would-be artist had painted a spray of flowers in the center which just didn't belong.

"Isn't this gorgeous? I've been wanting to show you my antique tôle because I knew you'd appreciate it." This piece was exquisite, ornamented by an expert, but it was a reproduction decorated in the old manner. There was no justification for labeling it "tôle," a term that refers to French painted ironware, perhaps tinned. There was nothing wrong with this reproduction except my hostess' misconception of its age.

IDENTIFICATION OF OLD TINWARE

One expects the antique dealer and other antiquarians, who through association often appear to qualify as experts, to be able to distinguish between the old and the new. Although it does take considerable handling to be able to differentiate easily between the well-preserved old piece, the cleverly redone old piece, and the reproduction with the fine old pattern, careful observation based on a few ground rules makes identification possible.

Once redecorated, old and new tinware are almost identical. Today's tinsmiths are using old patterns and doing painstakingly accurate work. This may be a clue—perhaps their work is too careful, for such inaccuracies as off-center hand holes have a charm all their own and remind us that originally tinware was made by men, not machines. Also, the metal used today in small pieces is often heavier than that used years ago. Some reproductions are made from sheet steel rather than tin-plated metal.

To separate the new from the old, start with the background paint. If the decoration is the country-tin type, the background will probably be japan paint, tar-based and lustrous. This paint is usually thinner at seams where one can see light streaks. Since it is thin and runs easily, "drapes" in the varnish are frequent. The background is apt to feel rough to the touch because of specks of dirt that settled before the finish dried. One coat of japan paint is honey-colored; more coats, baked at high heat, are black, and shades of bronze run the gamut between. (This finish was usually kiln-dried.)

Accurate copies of original country-tinware designs by members of The Historical Society of Early American Decoration.

It is rare for old japan painted tinware not to be scratched, for this varnish forms a brittle surface which marks readily. Since it is thin, it also rubs off at points of wear. I have seen a coffeepot with multiple designs almost intact, the japan paint completely worn off.

Colored backgrounds are usually oil based. (An exception is a Prussian-blue tinted varnish used with stenciled decoration.) Tinware with a background of oil-based paint sometimes shows its age by "alligatoring." This refers to crazing —hairline cracks in the surface of the paint— aggravated by age and heat. The same two factors may cause oil-paint designs to alligator, especially if the paint used was quite thick. In the Pennsylvania State Museum there is a well-preserved red coffeepot. Its bottom is raised by a flange and this flange is blackened, the paint patterned with heat cracks, showing that the pot was placed directly over heat, an infrequent practice. Most often coffee was boiled in a utilitarian pot, then served in a fancy one. Oil-based paint, heavier than japan paint, is also apt to flake off when it is dried by age or loosened by moisture.

Old-time decoration looks more professional than most modern painting, not because each stroke is perfect, but because the design seems to flow. It looks spontaneous; today's designs, all too often, look as if a decorator were following a pattern, as he probably is. Modern craftsmen love perfection and attempt it with each stroke. This may result in too-perfect, artificial appearance. The early flowerers left borders off single ends of document boxes, forgot to wipe off smudges and were far less meticulous about striping and brush-stroking than today's trained painters.

Colors on old pieces are bright when they are clean although many times upon discovery they are dimmed by the dirt of a century or more.

Butler deed box with graceful brush strokes, expertly rendered. Collection of the author.

Sometimes modern decorators, attempting to imitate the antique, dull their colors unrealistically. It is true that occasional color on early ware appears to have oxidized and darkened. This is exemplified particularly by greens, sometimes so dark they are hard to distinguish from the background.

Country-painted tinware does not have a protective coat of varnish. Fancier tea trays, however, were varnished, sometimes only over the pattern. These were tediously pumiced and revarnished alternately until an effective cover coat was built up. An account of the Tea Tray Works in Greenwich, New York, refers to women using pumice and oil who polished trays with the heels of their hands until the skin was worn smooth. Another report describes the salvage of decorated tinned ironware from the ocean after a ship sank while en route from Britain to Holland. Reputedly the ware although underwater for about a year, was found intact.

EUROPEAN WARE

Many of the more elaborate trays, urns, caddies, etc. were European, although, of course, not all. Philadelphia, Boston, and New York boasted a roster of japanners, some listed in newspapers as "newly-arrived" from Britain. Many of the japanners, though, ornamented furniture or vehicles (coaches and sleighs) rather than metalware. Numerous newspaper advertisements announced the sale of both imported and domestic decorated ware. A few shapes are characteristic of English or Welsh tin- or ironware. One is the pierced-edge or lace-edge tray, which may be round, oval, or rectangular. The painting peculiar to these trays is done in oils, and on the best pieces, is especially delicate. Motifs are apt to contain fruit, birds, or flowers, alone

Dainty Butler pattern with especially fine brush-stroking on top. Number of stripes on front of cover unusual. Courtesy of James Stevens, Greenville, New York.

or in combination. The greens used in leaves have a bluish tinge, and white built-up highlights are evident throughout the design. Ordinarily there is a fine gold-leaf border around the floor of a pierced-edge tray although this may have worn off completely. Caddies, boxes, and teapots also may duplicate lace-edge designs.

So-called Chippendale and Queen Anne trays with scalloped edges were popular in England and Wales. Such trays in varying sizes were sometimes painted in sets. Painting on fine examples of this type demanded a high degree of skill. Oils, bronze powders, and gold leaf were the media employed, sometimes separately, oftentimes combined on a single piece. Some designs done entirely in gold leaf were exquisitely detailed; oil-painted patterns resembled the best still-life canvases of the period. Again, tea trays or "boards" were most plentiful, but other Chippendale-painted pieces, such as caddies and teapots, were produced.

Tin, iron, and papier-mâché wares were made in quantity in Usk and Pontypool, Wales; in Wolverhampton and Birmingham, England. The latter city was known for its oval trays, many of which were ornamented with mother-of-pearl. Frequently such trays were molded from papier-mâché although this material was pressed into a variety of shapes. Even card tables and chairs were papier-mâché. Tilt-top tables and beds were fabricated. The suggestion that papier-mâché be used to construct bridges and buildings did not receive popular support, however. Much of the papier-mâché found in America today is Oriental, a highly commercial product of the twentieth century.

There was apparently no deluge of genuine tôle (French decorated ironware) in America during the eighteenth and nineteenth centuries although today importers of antiques are exhibiting quantities of tôle. Most of the French ware now found in this country, has, I believe, come over during this century and continues to be brought in annually as antique dealers and interior decorators make their regular buying trips abroad. Wine coolers, pairs of vases, student lamps, and trays from France are ornamented with classical figures in gold leaf or with pastoral scenes in the manner of the practiced genre artist; some early French decoration was achieved by decalcomania.

CARE OF TINWARE

Country-tin decoration, distinctive in its characteristics, is of particular interest to Americans, because, like jazz, it seems to have blossomed from old country roots into something uniquely a part of this country. If you are blessed with a piece of antique tinware in fine condition, these hints may help you to keep it that way.

1. Cleanse the piece carefully with mild soap and lukewarm water. Remember that if there is no varnish, a heavy hand may remove such details as fine brush-strokes.

2. Apply a thin coat of clear, high-grade varnish. (Some collectors prefer wax without varnish, but an added finish of some sort will seal and brighten.)

3. Continue to keep the piece waxed or polished with a good furniture polish.

If your heirloom needs restoration, find an artist skilled in the arts of the old-time decorator who will know exactly what to do with it. Tinware that has survived this long deserves tender preservation.

Glossary

ALIZARIN CRIMSON: deep red shade of oil paint

ALLIGATORING: crazing of a painted surface so that it resembles an alligator's hide; caused by heat and age.

BLOCK TIN: a kind of pewter

BRONZING: decorating with bronze powders

COUNTRY PAINTING: type of freehand decoration on tinware

COUNTRY TIN: tinware that bears country painting—usually deed boxes, canisters, caddies, octagonal trays, and such pieces

CRYSTALLIZED TINWARE: tinware that has been made from plate which was treated with acid until crystals showed in surface plating

FLANGE: rolled outer edge of tray

FLOWERING: old name for decorating country tin

GILDING: applying gold leaf

JAPANNED WARE: tinware or ironware that has been painted with a background of japan varnish

JAPANNING: the art of applying varnish-like japan lacquer

JOURNEYMAN: tinsmith who has finished his apprenticeship but not yet become a master smith employing others

LAND OF STEADY HABITS: Connecticut

NUTMEG STATE: Connecticut

PEDDLER'S NEWS: stale news

PEDDLER'S PONY: a walking stick

PIERCED TINWARE: tinware that has been pierced by chisels, usually in a design; purpose may be utilitarian or decorative

PLANISHED WARE: ware made from hammered tinplate

POLTERGEIST: a friendly ghost

PUNCHED TINWARE: ware made from tinplate which has been hammered with special tools so that bosses form designs

STAKE: form over which tinware is shaped

STATE OF BLUE LAWS: Connecticut

STEELYARDS: scales used by peddlers to weigh barter

SWEDGE: tool used to make ridges in tinware

TEABOARD: tray

TIN KNOCKER: tinsmith

TINPLATE WORKER: tinsmith

TINSNIPS: tin shears

TÔLE: ironware decorated in France

WAITER: tray

WEATHERCOCK: weathervane

WRIGGLED WARE: tinware that has been incised with a fine chisel usually in a delicate design

YELLOW OCHRE: brownish-yellow shade of oil paint

Bibliography

There would have been little to say that had not been said before had I not found a number of primary sources for *The History and Folklore of American Country Tinware.* These are the original documents, account books, diaries, business papers, and letters, which have proved invaluable:

Brandow ledger: New-York Historical Society, New York, New York
Minerva Butler Miller album: New York State Historical Association, Cooperstown, New York
Correspondence of Charlotte Wray: author's collection
Drowne day book: American Antiquarian Society, Worcester, Massachusetts
Eicholtz day book: Historical Society of Pennsylvania, Philadelphia, Pennsylvania
Filley correspondence and ledgers: Connecticut State Library and Miss Dorothy Filley Bidwell, Hartford, Connecticut
Thomas Haywood ledger: Connecticut State Library
Robert Henderson account book: New York City Public Library
William Holbrook diary: New York State Library, Albany, New York
Judd manuscripts: Forbes Library, Northampton, Massachusetts
Ledger of anonymous smith: New York State Historical Association, Cooperstown, New York
North family papers: Charles F. Montgomery collection
North tool-makers' ledger: Yale University, Library, New Haven, Connecticut
Morillo Noyes papers: Baker Library, Harvard University, Cambridge, Massachusetts
Parsons and Whiting papers: Dedham Historical Society, Dedham, Massachusetts
Thompson General Store papers: Pennsylvania State Library, Harrisburg, Pennsylvania

I have also studied the tinware designs included in the Index of American Design at the National Gallery of Art, Washington, D.C., and the folklore files of Dr. Louis Jones and the late Dr. Harold W. Thompson.

Adams, Ruth: *Pennsylvania Dutch Art.* Cleveland: World Publishing Co., 1950.
Ainsworth, Lillian M.: "The Tin Peddler," *Granite Monthly,* Nov. 1928.
Andrews, Dana E.: *The Gift to be Simple.* New York: J. J. Augustin, 1940.
Arnold, F. S.: "Our Old Poets and Tinkers," *American Folklore Journal,* vol. 2.
Avery, E. C.: "Sculptor and Weathervane Maker," *Monitor,* 1931.
Axon, W. E.: *Biographical Note of Ann Lee.* Liverpool: T. Brakell, 1876.
Bailey, Henry D. B.: *Local Tales and Historical Sketches.* Fishkill Landing: Spaight, 1874.
Baker, Muriel L.: "The Pattisons of Berlin," *The Decorator,* vol. 8, no. 2.
Barnum, P. T.: *The Life of P. T. Barnum.* New York: Redfield, 1855.
Beecher, Catherine: *A Treatise on Domestic Economy.* New York: Harper and Brothers, 1859.
Beers, J. B.: *History of Greene County.* New York: Beers, 1884.
Bishop, J. Leander: *History of American Manufactures,* 2 vols. Philadelphia: E. Young and Co., 1868.
Blackington, Alton: "Cling Clang, the Vaulting Pedlar," *Yankee,* Feb. 1956.
Book of Prices of Journeymen's Wages for Making Tin-ware. Philadelphia: 1796.
Botkin, Benjamin A.: *A Treasury of American Folklore.* New York: Crown, 1944.
Brazer, Esther Stevens Fraser: "Butler Tinware," *Antiques,* Aug. 1945.
——: *Early American Decoration.* Springfield, Mass.: Pond-Ekberg, 1940.
——: "Tinsmiths of Stevens Plains," Parts 1 and 2, *Antiques,* June and Sept. 1939.
——: "Zachariah Brackett Stevens," *Antiques,* Mar. 1936.

Brinkerhoff, Thomas: *Historical Sketch of the Town of Fishkill*. Fishkill Landing: Dean and Spaight, 1866.

Brown, Ruth T.: "The Tin Peddler," *The Decorator*, vol. 5, no. 2.

Butts, I. R.: *The Tinman's Manual*. Boston: I. R. Butts & Co., 1861.

Cabinet Maker's Guide. London: 1825.

Carson, Gerald: *The Old Country Store*. New York: Oxford University Press, 1954.

"Children of the Church," *The New York Evangelist*, Jan. 16, 1845.

Christensen, Erwin O.: *The Index of American Design*. New York: Macmillan, 1950.

Cooper Union: *Chronicle of the Museum for the Arts of Decoration*, vol. 2, no. 3.

Colonial Society of Massachusetts: *Publications*, vols. 6, 14.

Crisfield, V. Johnson: *History of Washington County*. 1878.

DeVoe, Shirley Spaulding: "The Upson Tin and Clock Shops," *The Connecticut Historical Society Bulletin*, July 1961.

Dolan, J. R.: *The Yankee Peddlers of Early America*. New York: Clarkson N. Potter, 1964.

Dunbar, D. E.: *The Tinplate Industry*. Boston: Houghton Mifflin, 1915.

Dunn, James: " 'The Murdered Pedlar' and the Saugerties Bard," *New York Folklore Quarterly*, vol. 11, no. 2.

Dwight, Timothy: *Travels in New England and New York*, vol. 4. New Haven: 1822.

Eaton, Ethel: "Any Rags?" *Christian Science Monitor*, Feb. 20, 1943.

Ebblewhite, E. A.: *A Chronological History of the Worshipful Company of Tinplate Workers Alias Wire Workers of the City of London*. London.

Eberlein, Harold Donaldson, and McClure, Abbot: *The Practical Books of Early American Arts and Crafts*. Philadelphia: J. B. Lippincott, 1916.

Elliott, Ella Z.: *Old Schuylkill Tales*. Pottsville, Pa.: pub. by the author, 1906.

Everest, Charles: *The Poets of Connecticut with Biographical Sketches*. Hartford: Case, Tiffany and Burnham, 1843.

Flick, Alexander: *History of the State of New York*, vol. 8. New York: Columbia University Press, 1949.

Flint, Timothy: *Recollections of the Last Ten Years*. Boston: Cummings, Hilliard and Co., 1826.

Forbes, Allan: *Towns of New England and Old England, Ireland and Scotland*. New York: Tudor Publishing Co., 1920.

Foulke, Roy: *The Sinews of American Commerce*. New York: Dun and Bradstreet, 1941.

Freedley, Edwin: *Philadelphia and Its Manufactures in 1857*. Philadelphia: E. Young, 1858.

French, J. H.: *Historical and Statistical Gazetteer of New York State*. Syracuse: R. P. Smith, 1860.

Fuller, R. H. *Jubilee Jim*. New York: Macmillan, 1928.

Gallt, F.: *Dear Old Greene County*. Catskill: 1915.

Gardner, E. E.: *Folklore from the Schoharie Hills*. Ann Arbor: University of Michigan Press, 1937.

Goodale, S. L.: *Chronology of Iron and Steel*. Cleveland: Penton Publishing Co., 1931.

Gould, Mary Earle: *The American House*. New York: Medill-McBride, 1949.

——: *Antique Tin and Tole Ware*. Rutland, Vt.: Charles E. Tuttle, 1958.

Gottesman, Rita: *The Arts and Crafts in New York, 1723-1776*. New York: New-York Historical Society, 1936.

Greene, W. H.: "An Extinct Manufacture—the Old Pontypool Japan Ware," *The Art Journal*, 1872.

Guild, Calvin: "Connecticut Corner, Dedham, before 1910," *Dedham Historical Register*, vol. 5.

Guild, James: "From Tunbridge, Vermont, to London, England," *Proceedings, The Vermont Historical Society* (new series) vol. 5, no. 3 (1937).

Guinn, J. M.: *Historical and Biographical Record of Monterey and San Benito Counties*. Los Angeles: Historical Record Co., 1910.

Hale, Edward E.: *Historical Boston*. New York: D. Appleton & Co., 1903.

Hall, A. N.: "Old Wholesale Peddler and His Teams," *New England Magazine*, Aug. 1900.

Harris, A. B.: "Old Time Pedlars," *The Granite Monthly*, 1877.

Hawthorne, Nathaniel: *American Notebooks*. Boston: Houghton Mifflin, 1899.

——: "Drowne's Wooden Image," *Mosses from an Old Manse*. Boston: Desmond Publishing Company, 1900.

Hayward, Arthur: *Colonial Lighting*. New York: Dover Publications, 1962.

Hind, C. Lewis: *Days in Cornwall*. New York: Brentano's, 1907.

Hodgson, Mrs. Willoughby: "The Art of Japanning," *Antiques*, Mar. 1929.

Humphrey, Zephrine: *A Book of New England*. Boston: Hewell, Soskin, 1947.

John, W. D.: *Pontypool and Usk Japanned Wares*. Newport, England: Ceramic Book Company, 1953.

Jones, Louis C.: *Things That Go Bump in the Night*. New York: Hill and Wang, 1959.

Kauffman, Henry J.: *Early American Copper, Tin and Brass*. New York: Medill-McBride, 1951.

——: *Pennsylvania Dutch American Folk Art*. New York: American Studio Books, 1946.

Keir, Malcolm: "The Unappreciated Tin Peddler," *Journal of Political Economy*, vol. 21.

Kendall, Edward Augustus: *Travels Through the Northern Parts of the United States in the Years 1806-1807*. New York: I. Riley, 1809.

Kline, P. C.: "New Light on the Yankee Peddler," *New England Quarterly*, vol. 12.

Lassiter, William: "The Shaker Legacy," *House and Garden*, Mar. 1945.

Lichten, Frances: *Folk Art of Rural Pennsylvania*. New York: C. Scribner's Sons, 1946.

Lipman, Jean: *American Folk Art*. New York: Pantheon, 1948.

Long, Theodore: *Tales of the Cocolannus*. New York: W. Neale, 1914.

Lutes, Della: "Parade of the Peddlers," *American Mercury*, Sept. 1940.

Maxwell, Col. A. M.: *A Run Through the United States, During the Autumn of 1840*. London: 1841.

McClinton, Katherine: *Antique Collecting*. New York: McGraw-Hill, 1951.

Melcher, Marguerite: *The Shaker Adventure*. Princeton: Princeton University Press, 1941.

Millenial Laws. New Lebanon: 1821.

Milliman, Marjorie: "Who Said 'The Last of the Tin Pedlars'?" *The Decorator*, vol. 4, no. 1.

Mills, Lewis, Jr.: "Connecticut Manufacturing," *The Lure of the Litchfield Hills*, vol. 28.

Mitchell, Edwin V.: *The Romance of New England Antiques*. New York: A. M. Wyn, 1950.

Mundey, A. H.: *Tin and the Tin Industry*. London: Sir I. Pitman and Sons, 1925.

Munsell, Joel: *Annals of Albany*, 1871.

North, C. M.: *History of Berlin, Connecticut*. New Haven: The Tuttle, Morehouse & Taylor Co., 1916.

North, Dexter: *John North of Farmington, Connecticut and His Descendants*. Washington, D.C.: 1921.

North, Helen M.: "The Tin-Peddler's Cart," *The New England Magazine* (new series) vol. 20.

Ormsbee, Thomas H.: "The Peddler, an Early American Institution," *Collector*, Mar. 1945.

Phillips, George: "Connecticut Corner," paper read before the Dedham Historical Society.

Porter, Edward G.: *Rambles in Old Boston*. Boston: Cupples, Upham and Co., 1887.

Pratt, Reverend Magee: "Berlin, a Sketch," *Connecticut Magazine*, Jan. 1900.

Price, E. L.: "The Art of Lacquering," *Antiques*, Nov. 1932.

Ralph, J.: "A Trip with a Tin Pedlar," *Harpers*, Apr. 1903.

Rawson, Marion Nicholl: *Candleday Art*. New York: E. P. Dutton, 1938.

Ritter, Abraham: *Philadelphia and Her Merchants*. Philadelphia: Ritter, 1860.

Robacker, Earl: "The Case for Pennsylvania German Tin," *Antiques*, Oct. 1947.

——: *Pennsylvania Dutch Stuff.* Philadelphia: University of Pennsylvania Press, 1944.

Robacker, Earl, and Boyd, E.: "Decorated Tinware East and West," *Antiques*, Sept. 1954.

Robinson, Everett N.: "The Country Tin of Oliver Filley." *The Decorator*, vol. 2, no. 2.

Rowe, Ernest: *Highlights of Westbrook History.* Portland.

Salem's Sons and Daughters: *The Salem Book.* 1896.

Scharf, H.: *The History of Westchester County*, vol. 1, 1886.

Scrapbook Clippings. Schenectady Historical Society.

Sears, Clara: *Gleanings from Old Shaker Journals.* Boston: Houghton Mifflin, 1916.

Seybolt, R. F.: *Apprenticeship and Apprenticeship Education in Colonial New England and New York.* New York: Teachers' College, Columbia University, 1917.

Shaw, S. M.: *History of Cooperstown.* 1886.

Shepherd, Odell: *Pedlar's Progress.* Boston: Little, Brown & Company, 1937.

Stackpole, Everett: *Old Kittery and Her Families.* Lewiston, Maine: Press of Lewiston Journal, 1903.

Standard Dictionary of Folklore. 2 vols. New York: Funk and Wagnalls, 1949-50.

Staples, A. G.: "Old Peddler's Cart," *Old Time New England.*

State of New York: *Peddlers' Licenses.* 4 vols., 1840-1886.

Steinman Hardware Company: *Two Hundred Years of the Hardware Business.* Lancaster, Pa.: 1944.

Stowe, Charles Messer: "Ann Butler's Painted Tinware—First Signed Work Discovered," *New York Sun*, Mar. 11, 1933.

Stroudt, J. J.: *Pennsylvania Folk Art.* Allentown, Pa.: Schlechter's, 1948.

Swan, Mabel: "The Village Tinsmith," *Antiques*, Mar. 1928.

Thompson, Harold W.: *Body, Boots and Britches.* Philadelphia: Lippincott, 1940.

Tudor, Henry: *Narrative of a Tour in North America.* London: 1834.

Vedder, Jessie *Official History of Greene Country.* Catskill, New York: 1927.

Wadsworth Atheneum: *Tin, Today and Yesterday.* Mar. 1945.

Wallace, David H., and Groce, George C.: *Dictionary of Artists in America 1564-1860.* New Haven: Yale University Press, 1957.

Washington, George: "Household Accounts," *Pennsylvania Magazine*, vol. 35.

Webb, Wheaton: "Peddler's Protest," *New York State History*, 1943.

Weeks, Pearl: *History of Hartwick.* Hartwick Reporter, 1934.

Weise, A. J.: *History of Lansingburg.* Troy: W. H. Young, 1877.

Weishaar, Wayne, and Parrish, Wayne: *Men Without Money.* New York: G. P. Putnam's Sons, 1933.

"The Welcome Traveling Bazaar," *Scrapbook Clippings.* Schenectady Historical Society.

Weston, George F., Jr.: "The Vanes of Boston," *New York Folklore Quarterly*, vol. 13. (Reprinted from *Boston Ways: by and Folk.*)

Weygandt, Cornelius: *The Dutch Country.* New York: D. Appleton Co., 1939.

——: *The Red Hills.* Philadelphia: University of Pennsylvania Press, 1929.

Whitney, James S.: *Apprenticeship and a Boy's Prospect of a Livelihood.* Philadelphia: 1872.

Windsor, Justin: *Memorial History of Boston.* Boston: J. R. Osgood and Co., 1881.

Woodside, Charles and Lura: "Three Maine Pewterers," *Antiques*, July 1932.

Wright, Richardson: *Hawkers and Walkers in Early America.* Philadelphia: Lippincott, 1927.

Yates, Raymond: *The Hobby Book of Stencilling and Brush Stroke Painting.* New York: McGraw-Hill, 1951.

I studied many old newspapers, including, for instance, The *Lansingburg* (New York) *Democrat, Lansingburg* (New York) *Gazette, Portland* (Maine) *Argus, Deering* (Maine) *News, Freeman's Journal* (Cooperstown, New York), *Massachusetts Gazette and Boston Weekly News-Letter.*

Appendix I

Process of tinplating used in Britain (from D. E. Dunbar's *The Tinplate Industry*)

1. The iron slabs are heated five times and rolled in five stages. Rolling of sheet bar into a pack of thin sheets is a laborious task needing skilled workmen. Temperatures in the mill are high, and since the fires are always kept burning, men work in three eight-hour shifts.

2. When rolled packs are cool, they pass to shearmen to be cut to desired size. Shears are driven by gears from the main shaft of the mill and are always in operation. Besides skilled workmen, a boy called a "behinder" works here bundling scrap.

3. Sheets have become slightly welded, so they pass now to an opener's bench, where women tear the sheets apart with pieces of metal in the palms of their hands.

4. Girls pack sheets into cradles which are lowered into vats, one of sulphuric acid and one of water. The girls then unpack the vats. The pickling department is generally a dirty and unwholesome place. The workers are exposed to wet floors, acid fumes, and general humidity due to vapors from the pickling vats.

5. At this stage sheets are brittle. They become tough and hardened through annealing. Sheets are rolled again with greater pressure to give a smoother surface. The sheets are fed and carried back and forth by little boys and girls.

6. Sheets are next dipped into boiling palm oil, then into molten tin. They are usually dipped into the tin three times, then into a pot of grease.

7. While still hot, the tin-plated sheets are polished by girls using sheepskins. Sheets are now ready to be sorted and packed.

Appendix II

HISTORICAL BACKGROUND

EARLY USE OF TIN

The earliest known use of tin was among the Egyptians in about 3000 B.C. We are told that ornaments and utensils at this time were made from alloys containing tin. Tombs of the XVIIIth Dynasty have yielded a ring and a pilgrim bottle of pure tin, the earliest objects made from the unalloyed metal which have been found. The Old Testament Hebrew word "bedhil" is translated "tin" and Joseph of Arimethea, benefactor of Jesus, supposedly gained his wealth trading in tin from the British Isles. This was Britain's first export, and the Phoenician sailor-traders who traveled there called the British Isles the "Isles of Tin." Herodotus commented on the tin trade in 450 B.C. He tells the story of a Phoenician captain pursued by a Roman ship who ran his galley on the rocks rather than disclose his cargo to an enemy who might guess its origin. Greeks and Romans, too, eventually did follow the Phoenicians to Britain and a translation from the Greek poet Homer notes the use of tin in making Achilles' shield:

> Ten rows of azure steel the work unfold;
> Twice ten of tin, and twelve of ductile gold.

In Britain, tin ore was mined from veins in the rocky bluffs of Cornwall at the tip of the peninsula which resembles a bony finger pointing into the English Channel. Even today mole-like ponies and their masters still gather casserite or "tinstone" beneath the surface of these same cliffs.

TINPLATE

Tinplate, from which tinwares are actually made, is a thin sheet of iron coated with tin. The process of plating was evolved to prevent rust. Tinplating of already-shaped iron implements was practiced by the Romans (Pliny mentions such plating) and was introduced into Britain during the Roman occupation. Still, the manufacture of sheets of tinplate was not accomplished commercially until about 1530 in Bohemia. During the seventeenth century tinplating works appeared in Saxony, Alsace, Germany proper, and Britain. These early factories were crude and unpleasant; their existence was uncertain; their efforts, experimental.

In Britain, the Hanbury Iron Works was one of the first established, and here tinplating was practiced. These works were in Pontypool, a town founded by the Hanbury family in Monmouthshire which has been described as "the English County . . . (which) jabs an elbow into the rocky ribs of Wales." Thomas Thomas, who kept the Pontypool Punch House and thought himself a poet, described the making of tinplates:

> . . . Your fathers from afar,
> First brought the art to bend the massive bar;
> 'Tween massive rolls its serpent formt to glide,
> 'Till plates elastic show their purple side;

In heated pots the Cambrian silver glows,
And quick o'er satin sheets it smoothly flows,
When to the astonished isle they soon present
What none but they or angels could invent. . . .

Later Queen Victoria's Inspector of Factories for Wales visited several plating factories and reported with distaste:

Rubbish of old iron, disused machinery of all sorts and shapes, rubbish of wood, of bricks, of coal, of shearings, are everywhere. You lift your eyes and find your field of sight intersected perpendicularly, horizontally, diagonally, in every sort of direction, by uprights supporting the roof, by steam pipes reaching from wall to wall, now high up, now very little over your head, by oscillating beams, by flues of furnaces, by elevations of all sorts of shapes, but all black. . . . Whether a tin-plate works be old or new, neither is the immediate neighborhood, or the inside, a place to linger in. . . .

JAPANNING

Thomas Allgood, who became manager of the Hanbury Works in the late seventeenth century, was the first in Britain to perfect the art of japan-painting. He created a varnish-like paint which, when applied to metal and kiln dried, simulated the finish of Oriental lacquer. This paint was called Japan-paint or merely "Japan." Today's asphaltum resembles "Japan," which produced a glowing, lustrous finish. At first applied directly to sheet-iron wares, Japan-paint served the same purpose as plating by preventing oxidation with its resultant rust and corrosion. Later this paint was used on wares made of tinplate. In 1734 Charles Hanbury wrote to his wife, "Tom Allgood has found a new way of japanning, which I think so beautiful that I'll send you a couple of pieces of it."

It was Edward Allgood, son of Thomas, who produced japanned goods in quantity. However, in 1761, a family quarrel split the Allgood family and one branch migrated to Usk where another factory was established. For the next hundred years, more or less, the manufacture of tinplates and tinwares, and the japanning and decorating of these wares was an important industry in both Wales and England.

DECORATION

Decoration of many English wares was expert. The trays featured by the Pontypool Japan Works were round ones, oval ones, and rectangular ones with glinting tortoise-shell backgrounds and pierced rims. Delicate flowers, birds, fruits, and sometimes portraits or scenes ornamented the centers of these Pontypool "waiters," while sprays of buds or similar designs surrounded the central motif. Dainty gold-leaf borders wound around the outside edge of the floor. Pontypool artisans also created graceful chestnut urns; they made bread and cheese trays, teakettles, tea caddies, and cake baskets with similar patterns and other intricate designs in gold leaf alone. Dr. Richard Pococke, Bishop of Meath, visited the Hanbury Works and described their wares in 1756:

Of a thicker plate they make salvers and candlesticks, and many other things which they Japan; I am told the lighter parts of this in imitation of tortoise shell is done with silver leaf. They adorn them with Chinese landscapes and figures in gold only, and not with colouring as in Birmingham, but it is dear, there being only two brothers and their children, who make it and keep it a secret.

Rural scenes, which resemble miniatures of oil paintings of the day, appear winding around coffee urns and teapots. Thatched roofed huts and churches, bridges, domestic animals, and rustics vie for interest in these busy scenes, which may have been copied from the paintings or engravings of one Barker of Bath, popular artist in the early part of the nineteenth century.

A "Mr. M." who toured Pontypool in 1801 made the intricate procedure of decorating sound commonplace—almost dull:

> We entered one of the manufactures of Japan ware that bears the name of Pontycool but it did not answer our expectations. The first coating of Japan is put on the tin or copper vessel which is then placed in an oven and at a fixed period taken out and polished. The ornaments are neatly drawn with a hair pencil and a particular size which when dried is covered with leaf Silver. It is again varnished, which changes the Silver into Gold, for they use not Gold leaf in any of their works. The process is very simple but tedious and we did not consider ourselves compensated for the journey.

In Usk fine gold-leaf borders were popular, and pattern books showing these borders ready for duplication are still in existence. Usk pieces sometimes carried all-over patterns; candleholders were studded with tiny gold stars; bun trays resembled sunbursts, with fine stripes radiating from the middle to the edges of the trays. "Stormant," undulating and seemingly never-ending lines in various metallic colors (perhaps named for a long-winded politician of the day), was particularly favored at Usk as were brown, buff, and maroon backgrounds.

During the eighteenth century and the beginning of the nineteenth, many japanning works other than those at Pontypool and Usk were established in England, some located at Wolverhampton, Clerkenwell, Bilston, Birmingham, and Windsor. Rectangular trays with gold-leaf borders and superimposed freehand bronze fruits and flowers were plentiful, as were the Gothic-or Chippendale-type trays. Heavy oval trays were also produced in quantity.

TÔLE

Britain had no monopoly on decorated tin and iron wares. The French produced many such pieces, and in addition sometimes japanned and decorated copper wares. The French wares only, decorated or undecorated, are properly identified as "tôle." In 1692, DePradel's *Livre Commode* mentions Frenchmen who painted in "la façon de Chine." Jaubert's *Dictionnaire des Artes et Métiers*, published about 1790, states:

> Painting of tôle is of very ancient use in Turkey. . . . In Italy, in England and in France and elsewhere efforts have been made to imitate this process of the Levant. . . . The first to succeed was a man who established himself in Rome forty years ago, the articles which he made were covered with a varnish which he claimed to be the real varnish of China, tested by fire.

By 1799, Citizen DeHarme exhibited painted tôleware at the first Exposition of Industrial Arts in Paris and his work was highly praised:

This ingenious artist has found a way to make vases of the most elegant form in varnished and gilded tôle. Even in the Grecian and Etruscan style and to decorate them with the most delightful and delicate ornaments. . . . The different types of vases, of which we can give only a suggestion . . . prove that the Citizen DeHarme has made the most of the discovery; and we do not hesitate to affirm that he has attained a degree of perfection far superior to that of foreign manufacture. . . . One finds in his shop everything from the "porte mouchette jusqu' à la baignoire."

At the Exposition held at the Louvre in 1819, Le Sieur Tavernier displayed his wares, articles of all colors "gilded and mounted in Bronze."

Some French decoration duplicated Oriental scenes painted in gold leaf; others, classic Greek scenes. Simon Martin, a royal coach-painter, was responsible for a unique finish used on metals. His varnish known by his name—Vernis Martin—was patented in 1744. It was used in an array of colors, often with flecks of gold suspended in the solution.

Wares similar to Japan ware and tôle were produced in Holland and Germany but not in as great quantities as in France.

It was logical that the colonists who migrated to America included tinsmiths and artisans from Britain and France and later from Germany and other European countries. Gradually a distinctly American tinware industry evolved, which the preceding text treats by discussing the smiths, decorators, and pedlars of these wares.

Index

*Numbers in italic type refer to pages
on which there are illustrations.*

acorn pattern, *84*
Adriance, Mrs. Howard
　(collector), *130, 133, 142,
　198*
Adams, G. (peddler), 118
Adams, Warren (peddler), 118
agents for North's tools, *66*
agreements, between peddlers
　and smiths, 74, 75, 78, 79,
　152-153
Albany, N.Y., 51, 66, *110, 126,
　130*
Alcott, Bronson (peddler), 60-
　61, 74-75
Alderman, Manna (peddler),
　61
American Antiquarian Society
　Library, 36
anniversary, tin, 25
　certificate, 27
anvils, use of, 14
apple trays, 77, 162
apprentices, 49-56, 153-154
Apprentices' Companion, The
　56
Augusta, Me., *92*
Austin, William (tinman), 66
Avery, Anne (collector), 77

Babb, Conrad (smith), 150
Babbitt, Tabitha, 125
Backus, Henry (poet), 196-197
Bailey, William (tinman), 109,
　151-152
Baker, Joseph (smith), 153
Baker, Library, Harvard Uni-
　versity, *94, 119,* 169, *170*
Ballston Spa, N.Y., 97
Baltimore, Md., 66
Barnes, Augustus (inventor), 64
Barnum, P. T., 180, 185-186
Barrett, Ben, story about, 187
barter, for tinware, 91, 94, 95-98,
　118, 173-174, 176-178
basins, price of, 158
basket, as decoration on box,
　130
Batavia, N.Y., 77
Beasom, Mike (peddler), 149-
　150
Beckley, Elias (toolmaker), 58
Beckley, Orrin (toolmaker),
　136
Bellows Falls, Vt., 67, 200
Bennett, Mrs. ——
　(decorator), 81

Benneville, M. de, 148
Bennington, Vt., potteries, 177
Berlin, Conn., 18, 56-57, 58,
　76-77, 81, 82, 90, 98, 108,
　135, 169
Berks County, Pa., 150, 161
Berkshire Center, Vt., 176
Betty lamps, 29
Bidwell, Miss Dorothy Filley,
　17
birds, on painted ware, 163,
　165
　on wriggled ware, 161, *164*
Bloomfield, Conn., 58, 82, 113
Bly, Dr. John, 128
Boas, Jacob (smith), 156, 157
bobbins, Shaker, 125
bonnets, of tin, 25, 27
book-clip candle-holder, *32, 32*
Book of New England, A, 47
Boonville, Mo., 26
Borst, Charles V. S., 18
Boston, Mass., 29
boxes, 101, *208; see also* candle
　boxes; deed boxes; docu-
　ment boxes; hat box; pill
　boxes; trinket boxes
Bradford, Joseph (tinman), 42
Bradley, Thomas (smith), 153
Brandow, Henry (tinman), 24
Brandy Hill, Greenville, N.Y.,
　131
Brazer, Esther Stevens, 91, 103,
　105-106, 201
brazier, charcoal, 14, *39*
bread tray, *86,* 162
　Butler, *127, 129, 132, 134*
　North, *138*
　Pennsylvania, *151, 154*
Bresee, Frank (peddler), 71-72
Briggs, —— (peddler), 102
Brinley, George, 47
Briscoe, Sarah Rose (decora-
　tor), 92, 103
Briscoe, Thomas (tinman), 92
British ware, 104-105, 165,
　207-208
bronzing, of tin, 79
"Brookfield 1845" (signature),
　106
Brown, Joseph Jr. (apprentice),
　78, 79
Brown, Luther (tinman), 114,
　115
Brown, William (?), 176
Brunson, Oliver (smith), 59

Bryn Mawr, Pa., *166*
buckets, price of, 157
Buckley, Allen (toolmaker), 64,
　65-66, 68
Buckley, Mary Ann
　(painter ?), 105
Buckley, Nancy (painter ?),
　105
Buckley, Oliver (tinman), 66,
　68, 93, 97, 105-106
Burch, John (tinman), 77, 109,
　111
Burlington, Vt., 96, 170
Burlington Democrat, 170
Butler, Abel, 128
Butler, Ann (signed box), *142,
　198*
　identifying her work, 163
Butler (Miller), Minerva, *115,
　130,* 133, 143
Butler family, Aaron, 17, 85,
　115, 127-134, 128, 131-134,
　207, 208
Byrd, William, 13

Cabinet Maker's Guide, The,
　162
caddy, *141, 152*
cages, 24, 25, 38
cake stamps, *see* cookie cutters
cake stand, *28*
Callendar, Levi (store owner),
　131
Cambridge, Mass., *94,* 119
Canada, peddlers in, 95, 111,
　118, 145
Canal Village, Mass., 68
candle boxes, 34
Candleday Art, 26
candle-holders, 26, 31, *31, 32,*
　34, 125
candlesticks, 152, 158, *176*
canister, 77
Cape Cod spout lamp, 30
care, of old ware, 210
Careless, Cotton and (japan-
　ners), 167
Carlisle, Pa., 151, 152
Carlisle Gazette, 151
cart, the murdered peddler's
　199
Carter and Fiske (peddlers), 73
carts, peddlers, *70, 71,* 72-73,
　107, 149
Carrington, "Doc" (merchant),
　187

Carson, William (smith), 156
Catskill, N.Y., 55, 190-191
Chambersburg, Md., 151
chandeliers, 33, 33-34, 34
chants, of tinkers, 179, 185
characteristics, of Butler decoration, 128-130, 133, 143-144
  of Maine decoration, 103-106, 116
  of New York State ware, 144-146
  of North decoration, 135, 137, 138, 139-143, 140-141
  of Pennsylvania ware, 163
"Charleytown," S.C., 66
Chateaugay, N.Y., 175
Chatham, N.Y., 107
cheese molds, 159
Cheritree, Buel (blacksmith), 131
Cheshire, Conn., 61, 62
Chester County, Pa., 150
chisels, use of, 14, 66
Christmas-tree candle-holders, 34
churns, 23
Cincinnati, Ohio, 61
Cling Clang (peddler), 98-100
clock case, of tin, 29
clothespins, wooden, used as change, 96
Cobble, Davis (tinman), 67
coffin-lid trays, 101, 105, 113, 162
coffeepots, 98, 109, 152, 157
  price of, 157, 158
  punched, 165
  signed, 83, 161, 190
  wriggled, 160, 164
colanders, 25, 120
collar box, 25
Colonial Lighting, 30
colors, distinctive, 89, 104, 140-141, 143-144, 145, 146
Connecticut, tinmen in, 49-87
Connecticut Historical Society Bulletin, The, 84
Connecticut State Library, 50, 54, 78, 80, 83
contracts, see agreements
Converse, Edward M. (inventor), 64
Cook, Captain, 38
cookie cutters, 23, 180
Cooperstown, N.Y., 24-26, 31, 37, 39, 70, 107, 125, 128, 134, 136, 137-138, 139, 141, 186
Cooper Union Museum, 84, 112
Cornish coast tin mines, 14
cornucopia, painted, 98, 104
Cornwall, Conn., 199
Cotton and Careless (japanners), 167

Coun and Company, T. M. (foundry), 115
Cowles, Joseph (tinman), 61
Cowles, Truman (tinman), 66
Crampten, —— (smith), 171, 176
Cravens Manufactory, James C. (shop), 167
cream jug, signed, 195
Crescent, N.Y., 197
crimping machine, 42
Cripton, "Blind" (peddler), 102-103
Croswell, William, 40
Crown Point, N.Y., 175
crystallized ware, 161-162
cups, price of, 158
cutting, of tin, 44-45

dairy utensils, 23
Danbury, Conn., 187
Dania, Fla., 16
Dash, John Baltus (tinman), 108
dates, on tinware, 84
Davis, Benjamin, 40
Davis, Samuel (smith), 155
Day, Nathan (smith), 53
daybook, of Eicholtz, 154-155
Dearborn, Mich., 25, 27, 181
decorated ware, early, 13
decoration, distinctive, Maine, 103-106
  of Butlers, 143-144
  of Filleys, 77, 81-85, 166
  Pennsylvania, 159-168
Dedham, Mass., 42-44, 77, 90, 108
Dedham Historical Society Library, 44
deed boxes, 73, 74, 76, 82, 83, 84, 85, 102, 108, 116, 175, 182
  Butler, 128, 129, 130, 131, 133
  New York State, 144
  North, 135, 137, 140
  Pennsylvania, 166
  Vermont, 172
Deerfield, Mass., 35, 40
Deering, Me., see Stevens Plains
Deering News, 103
Degenhardt, Henry (smith), 150
designs, copies of original, 204
Devoe, Shirley Spaulding, 84
DeWitt, Henry (Shaker worker), 123-124
Dick & Co., Dan'l (japanners), 167
dinner horns, 26
displaying old ware, 12
document boxes, see deed boxes
doll, peddler, 171

dolls, jointed, 26, 26
"dot" flowers, 115, 131, 140
"Drape and Swag" decoration, 76
drawer-pull handles, 166
Dresden, N.Y., 194, 195
Drowne, Shem (smith), 36-42
Drowne, Thomas (smith), 36
Drowne's Wooden Image, 38
drudging box, 22
drum, the murdered peddler's, 199
Drury, Bernice (collector), 82, 92, 102
Dunbar, —— (peddler), 118
Dunham, Elisha (tinman), 61, 81, 82
Dunham, Frederick (pewterer), 93
Dunham, Rufus (pewterer), 93, 95
Dutch Country, The, 167
Dwight, Rev. Timothy, 56-57 68-69, 188

Eads, Elder Harvey (Shaker), 124
ear-horns, 26
ear trumpet, 38
ears, for buckets, 117
East Greenville, N.Y., 128, 163
Easton, N.Y., 144
Edge, Mrs. (mattress mfr.), 176
education, of apprentices, 53
Ehninger, John Whetten (artist), 69
Eicholtz, Jacob (smith & painter), 154-156, 166-167
Elliot, Deacon Nathan, 55
Elliot, Frances (collector), 83, 109, 127, 144
Elliot, John (smith), 41
Elizabeth, N.J., 59
Eno, William (signed coffeepot), 83, 190
epaulet box, 25
Esterbrucks, Richard (smith), 41-42

Farmers Museum, The, 70
Featherbed Lane, Charlton, N.Y., 200
feathers, as barter, 118
fees, required of peddlers, 110, 111
Filley, Amelia (decorator), 84
Filley, Annis Humphrey, 59, 84
Filley, Augustus (smith), 59, 64, 66, 67, 83, 84, 112-118, 120-121
Filley, Edwin (tinman), 121

Filley, Harvey (smith), 59, 66, 75-76, 80, 81, 166
Filley, Lucius (smith), 59
Filley, Mr. and Mrs. Marcus, 17
Filley, Oliver Dwight Jr. (smith), 59, 64, 65
Filley, Oliver Sr. (tinman), 50, 53, 54, 55, 58-59, 64, 75, 78, 79, 80, 81, 117
Filley family (no given name), 25, 77, 83, 84, 86, 116, 145, 165
Fillmore, Oscar (peddler), 188
Finchour, Joseph (smith), 153
Fishkill, N.Y., 194-195
Fitzwilliam, N.H., 16
Flint, Timothy (author), 158
floating tinshop, 158-159
"flowering" of tinware, 77, 79, 81, 86, 89
Fly Creek, N.Y., 134
food safe, 159, 161
foot, of tin, 29, 101
foot warmers, 29, 159
Ford Museum, Henry, 25, 27, 181
Fox, Washington (murderer), 199
frames, for pictures, 26
France, ware from, 209-210
franchises, for Parsons-Whiting machines, 45-46
unwritten, 47
Francis, Edward (japanner), 82-83
Franklin, Benjamin, 30
Franklin, Josiah, 30
Franklin House, Rutland, Vt., 177
"Frederick-town," Md., 151
Freeman's Journal, The, 136, 186
Freiot and Company, S. (store), 120
French, Asa (tinman), 111
Fuller, Hial (peddler), 118
Fuller, Sara (collector), 166
fur pelts, as barter, 97, 118, 120

Gallup, Russell M. (tinman), 186
Garnaville, Iowa, 70
geometric designs, 143, 161
Georgetown, D.C., 158
ghost stories, peddlers, 192-200
Gilbert, D. (tinman), 161
Gilbert, Lyman (tinman), 66
Gilbert, William, 23
gilting, of tin, 77, 79
Glasgow, Donald (peddler), 48
Glens Falls, N.Y., 140
Gold Rush, 61

Goodrich, Asohet (tinman), 114, 115
goods, for peddling, 172-173
Graham, Francis (smith), 153
Graham, John (tinman), 108-109
Granby, Conn., 75
Grannis, John (smith), 62
Greenville, N.Y., 76, 85, 115, 116, 129, 130, 131, 132, 133, 134, 142, 144, 145, 175, 198, 208
Greenwich, N.Y., 207
Griswold, Hezekiah, 75
Guild, James (peddler), 120, 179, 180-182
guilds, of tinmen, 51

Hagerstown, Md., 151
Halifax, Vt., 179
Hall, Joseph P. (tinman), 114
Hallock, Isaac (hotel keeper), 131
hammers, smiths' 37, 65
Harding, Richard (merchant), 39
Harrington, Lyman (smith), 63
Harrisburg, Pa., 66, 156
Hart, Emma (poet), 57
Hartford, Conn., 50, 54, 78, 80
Harvard, Mass., 125
hat box, 25
hats 25, 27
Hawthorne, Nathaniel, 38, 47
Hays, Andrew (peddler), 75-76
Hayward, Arthur (author), 30
Hayward, Thomas (tinman), 22
Haywood, Thomas (tinman), 158
heart, on painted ware, 163
Heath, Emily (collector), 135
herb pan, on lamp, 30
Herkimer County, N.Y., 101-102
Hershey Estates Museum, The, 22, 161, 164
Hendry, Captain, 38
Henry, Edward Lamson (painter), 47
hides, as barter, 97
Historical Society of Early American Decoration, 17, 92, 101, 107, 204
Historical Society of Pennsylvania, 154
Hodgkins, Rev. Eleazor, 131
Holbrook, William (peddler), 169-170, 173-178
Holcomb, Hial (peddler), 118
Holt, Seth (peddler), 118

Horn, John (smith), 156
horns, 26, 38, 141
Horse Heaven Hill, legend of, 200
Horsefield, Israel (apprentice), 50, 53, 54, 55
Hubbard, —— (tinman), 81, 114
Hulbert, Miss (decorator), 81
Humphrey, Annis, 59
Humphrey, Hiram (smith), 59
Humphrey, Zephrine, 47
Hutter, Catherine, 18

identification, of old ware, 83-87, 140-141, 143, 203-210
illness, of peddlers, 73
Imlay, William H. (importer?), 115
indenture, see apprentices
indenture paper, 50
iron-works, first in U.S., 13

James, Henry (tinman), 64
japanning, 77, 79, 83, 85, 89, 109-111, 117, 140, 167, 205-206
Jefferson, Thomas, 158
Jerry Jingle Highway, Melrose, Mass., 201
Johnson, —— (tinman), 176
Jones, Dr. Louis, 18
Jonesville, Mich., 138
journeymen tinmen, 114
Judd, Ethan (smith), 59
jug, cream, signed, 195
syrup, Shaker, 126

Kellogg and Company, A. W. (foundry), 115
Kempton, Samuel (tinman), 109
Kendall, Augustus (author), 60
Kepner, William (smith), 156
kerosene cans, tin, 34
Ketterer, J. (tinman), 161
Key, Francis Scott, 158
King's Chapel, 29
Kingston, N.Y., 66
Kirtland, James (smith), 156
Koffman, Barney (peddler), 73

ladles, 152, 158
LaHue, Hiram (peddler), 71
Lake George, N.Y., 193
lamp fillers, 25, 123
lamps, 29-31
Lancaster, Pa., 154
Langdon, Barnabas (smith), 45
Lansingburg (Troy), N.Y., 59, 64, 66, 83, 112-118, 120-121
Lansingburg Gazette, 120
lanterns, 32-33, 34, 152, 155, 158
LaPrairie, Que., 111
Lassiter, William, 126
Lea, Zilla, 18

leaves, on Butler ware, 143
ledger, Shem Drowne's, 36
Lee, Ann (Shaker leader),
  121-122
Lee, Jared (smith), 59, 63
license, Vermont peddler's, *170*
lighting devices, 29-34, 35
Longfellow, Henry Wadsworth, 32
Lutes, Della (author), 72
Luzerne, N.Y., 187

machines, *65, 66; see also*
  Parsons—Whiting machines
  first patent for, 43-44
  improvements on original,
  63-64
Mackarthur, Duncan, 24
Madison, James, 43
mallets, wooden, 14
manufacture of tinplate,
  foreign, 12, 14
Mann, William (merchant), 39
Marion, Conn., 61
Marrott, Ted (tinker), *60*
Martin, Gina (collector), *92,
  157*
Martin, John (smith), 157-158
Martin, William (smith), 156
Massachusetts, early tinsmithing
  in, 35-48
*Massachusetts Gazette and the
  Boston Weekly News
  Letter,* 41
Massachusetts Historical
  Society, 36
materials, tinsmith's, 13
Matthews, Anson, 51
McKim, Nightingale (tinman),
  66
McKinley Tariff Act, 14
measures, price of, 158
Melcher, Marguerite, 126
mending tin, 39
metal junk, as barter, 97
Mickey, Julius (tinman), 21
milk pans, 23
Millenial Laws, of Shakers, 122,
  127
Miller, John (peddler), *130,*
  133-134
Miller, Joseph (tinman), 42
Miller, Minerva (decorator),
  115, 130, 133, *143*
Milliman, Julian (collector), *163*
Mills, John (peddler), 118
Mills, John (tinman), 111
Missouri Gazette, 26
Missouri Historical Society, 26
mittens, as barter, 118
Mobile, Ala., 61
molds, wooden, 38
Monroe, N.Y., 25, 27, 107

Montgomery, Dr. Charles, 169
Morrisania, N.Y., 24
Morrison, Jonathan (tinman),
  66
Morton, James (importer), 14
murder tales of peddlers, 147-
  148, 192-200
musicians, peddlers as, 71-72
mustard seed, as barter, 120
Mygatt, Hiram (japanner), *58,*
  82

names of places, 21, 200-201
Neal, Reuben (tinman), 26
Newark, N.J., Museum, *69*
Newell, Thomas (smith), 41
New Haven, Conn., 61
New Holland, Pa., 167-168
New Madrid, Mo., 158
news, carried by peddlers, 70
Newton, Daniel (inventor), 64
New York, N.Y., 51, 66, 71, *84,*
  107, 108-111, *112, 171*
*New-York Gazette and
  Weekly Mercury, The,* 14,
  108
New-York (City) Historical
  Society, The, *71,* 107, *171*
New-York Mercury, 108
New York State Historical
  Association, 24, 25, 26, 31,
  37, 39, 70, 107, 125, 137, 138,
  139, *141,* 169
New York State Library, *110*
"night hawk," 22
Niskayuna, N.Y., *120,* 121, *122,*
  124
No Head Hill, legend of, 200
Norfolk Va., 61
North, Albert (smith), 136,
  138, 139
North, Betsey (decorator), 139
North, Ceylon (tinman), 138
North, Edmund (toolmaker),
  68
North, Elijah (tinman), 93
North, Elisha (tinman), 93
North, Jedediah (toolmaker),
  51, 58, 66-68, 134, 136
North, Levi J. (circus owner),
  178
North, Linus (smith), 136-138
North, Lucy, 139
North, Mercy (decorator),
  135, *138,* 139-140
North, Norris (smith), 139
North, Stephen (tinman), 134,
  138
North Company, J. and E.
  (toolmakers), 68
North family (no given names),
  135, 138-143, 169
Norton, Vt., 102

Noyes, Morillo (tinman), *94,*
  96, 169-173
nursing bottle, infant's, *22, 25,
  155*

Old Deerfield, Mass., 35, 40
Old Fort (museum), 11
Old Museum Village, 25, 27, 107
Old South Church, Boston,
  Mass., 40
Old Sturbridge Village, *28,* 30,
  33, 34, 35, 37, *38, 42, 43,
  60,* 77, *83*
Old Tappan, N.J., 97
Oneonta, N.Y., 72
ornamented ware, forbidden to
  Shakers, 127
ornaments, Christmas-tree, 34
Osman, Maria (decorator), 187

Page, F. H. (trader), 177
painting of tinware, 79, 81-87,
  89, 92, *99,* 103-106, 117, 132,
  162-165, 167-168, 206-207
paints, price of, 117
Palmer, Mrs. Maxwell
  (collector), *134*
Palmyra, N.Y., 137
pans, Shaker, *126*
Parsons, Eli (smith), 42-46
papier-mâché, items of, 209
Parsons, Polly (decorator), *58,*
  77, 81
Parsons-Whiting tin machines,
  43-46, 62
Passmore, Thomas (smith), 153
patents, first, 43-45
patterns, for utensils, 14
Pattison (Paterson, Patterson),
  Edward (tinman), 56-58
Pattison, Shubael (tinman), *58,*
  98
pay, of workers, 77, 81, 85, 113,
  114, 115, 118, 152-153
Peck, Stowe, and Wilcox
  (machine company), 64
Peck family, Seth (tinman),
  62, 63, 64, 66
peddlers, 46-48, *47,* 68-76, *69, 70,
  71*
  Canadian, 95, 111, 118, 145
  fees required of, *110,* 111
  Filley, 117-118, 145
  life of a, 73-74
  Maine, 89, 93, 95-103, 106
  Noyes, 145, 170-171, 173-178
  stories about, 98-100, 147, 150,
  185-201
  travel to the South, 60, 61, 62
Pedler's Hill, Washingtonville,
  N.Y., 201
Pedlar's Bridge, New Rochelle,
  N.Y., 200

peg lamps, 30
Pemaquid Patent, 41
Pennsylvania, tinmen in, 147-168
Pennsylvania State Museum, 206
Penobscot Indians, 90
pepperbox, 22
perfection of Shaker ware, 124, 127
Peters, Hugh (poet), 191-192
petticoat lamps, 30
Pettis, Simon (tinman), 67
Philadelphia, Pa., 23, 51, 66, *86*, 147, 152, 154, *157*, 166, *182*, *190*
Philadelphia Museum of Art, *86*, 147, *157*, *182*, *190*
Phillips, Russell (peddler), 118
Pierce, Mrs. George (collector), *144*
piercing of tin panels, 60, 127, 151, 159-161
pill boxes, making, 65
Pittsburgh Gazette, 156
Plaisted, Captain, 38
"planished" ware, 153
plates, ABC's, 28
Poestenkill, N.Y., 199
poltergeist, the murdered peddler, 197, 199
"pony," peddler's, 72
poop light tin, 39
Poor, Marian (collector), *92*
Porter, Allen and Freeman (pewterers), 93
Porter, Elisha, story about, 186
Portfolio (magazine), 167
Portsmouth, N.H., 66
potteries, Bennington, Vt., 177
prices of ware, 155, 157-158
Prosser, Dr. Jonathan, 128
pumice, use of, 207
punched ware, 151, 159-161, *162*
punches, to cut tinplate, 64, 65-66

rags, as barter, 97, 120
Raiser, Jacob (smith), 153
Rawson, Marion, 26
Raymond, Charles (inventor), 64
Reading, Pa., 150
Recollections of the Last Ten Years, 158-159
reflectors, 31
Reitz, John (smith), 155
Revere, Paul, lantern, 32-33
Rhinecliff, N.Y., 199
Richardson, Francis B. (signed ware), *195*
Richards Hotel, Westport, N.Y., 177
Rick, Cornelius (tinker), 201

rivets, for tinware, 117
Robaker, Dr. Earl (collector), *23*
Robertson, Ione (collector), *140*
Robinson, "Yankee" (peddler), 190
Rochester, N.Y., 81
Rochester Museum of Arts and Sciences, 107
"Rock, The" (Shaker hymn), 122
Rock City Falls, N.Y., 16
rollers, for tin machine, 65
Rollins, Frank, 18
Root, William (smith), 59
roses, on Butler ware, 143
on Maine ware, 105
Roseumen, Richard (tinman), 109
Rounds, Ruby (collector), *128*
runaway apprentices, 56
Rupert, Vt., 200
Rutland, Vt., 16, 171, 176

Saint Johnsville, N.Y., 199
Saint Louis, Mo., 26, 64
Salem, Mass., 52-53
Salem, N.Y., 176
"sandbox," 22
Saugerties, N.Y., *83, 109, 127, 144,* 196
Saugus, Mass., 13
sausage stuffer, 23
saw, circular, designed, 125
Schenectady, N.Y., 28, 74
sconces, 31
Scott, Charlotte Wray, 70
Scott, Violet M. (collector), *172*
scratches, on old ware, 205-206
Scutt, Eli (farmer), 132
seams, in tinware, 14
Segar, Andrew (tinman), 66
shade, for candle, *163*
Shade, John (tinman), 161
Shade, P. (smith), 150-151, 161
Shaker Adventure, The, 126
Shaker Museum, 107
Shakers, *31, 32, 120,* 121-127, *122, 123, 125, 126*
shears, tinsmith's, 14, *37*, 65
Shedd, —— (tinman), 172
sheep skins, as barter, 120
Sheffield, Mass., 16
Shelburne, Vt., Museum, 107
shells, painted, 104
Shepherd, Odell (author), 74
shipment of tinplate, 116
shop, tin, 107
Shrimpton, Samuel, 39
signed ware, 83-84, *142, 143,* 161, *187, 195, 198*

signs, of the trade, 21
Simsbury, Conn., 58, 79, 81, 83
Smith, Eldad (smith), 59
Smith, Lester (inventor), 64
snips, *see* shears
snuffers, candle, 34
soldering iron, use of, 14
songs, of tinkers, 179, 182-183
South, peddlers in the, 60-62
Southington, Conn., 62, 63, 64
Southington, Sketches of, 63-64
spice pan, on lamp, 30
"spit box," 21
sponge-cake candlesticks, *31, 32*
Spook Bridge, Glenford, N.Y., 200
Spook Hollow, Milton, N.Y., 201
spout lamp, Cape Cod, 30
Springfield, Vt., *82, 92, 102*
squirrel cage, *24, 25*
Stafford, —— (tinman), 177
stakes, tinsmith's, 14, *38*, 65
stamps, making of, 53
stamping, machine for, 44
stars, Christmas-tree, 34
steam pot, Shaker, 125
Steele, Sam (tinker), 123
stencils, on tinware, 77, 79, 104
Stevens, Alfred (tinman), 91
Stevens, Cordelia, 91
Stevens, Emmaline, 91
Stevens, Isaac Sawyer, (blacksmith), 90
Stevens, James (collector), 18, *76, 85, 115, 116, 129, 131, 132, 144, 145, 175,* 208
Stevens, Miriam, 91
Stevens, Sally Briscoe, 105
Stevens, Samuel B. (tinman), 91
Stevens, Zachariah Brackett (tinman), 90-92, *99,* 103-104
Stevens family (no given names), 89-97
Stevens Plains, Me., 18, 66, 89-95, 97, *102,* 108
style of painting, *92, 97,* 103-106
Stewart, Sam (peddler), 190-191
stills, 26
Stonington, Conn., 83
stories about peddlers, 98-100, 147-150, 185-201
Stoughton, Jonathan (apprentice), 53
Stowe, Enos (inventor), 64
Stowe, Orson W. (inventor), 64
Sturbridge, Mass., *28, 30, 33, 34, 35, 37, 38, 42, 43, 60, 77, 83*

Sullivan, Me., 100
sundries, for peddlers to sell, 117, 172-173
swedges, used in tinwork, 65
Swinney, Holman J. (author), 193

table-tidy, 29-30
Tampa, Fla., 16
Tarrant, Mrs., 38
tazza, see cake stand
teakettles, Shaker, 126
teapots, 97, 125, 181
tea sets, of tin, 25, 28
Tea Trays Works, Greenwich, N.Y., 207
Ted, Peddler, 189
Temple, Joseph (merchant), 39
textiles, as barter, 118
  manufacturing, 98
Timlow, Herman (author), 63-64
Tin Cup, Colo., 201
tinder box, 26
Tinker Hill, Amsterdam, N.Y., 201
  Putnam County, N.Y., 201
Tinker Hollow, North Brookfield, N.Y., 201
tinkers, 179-183
Tinkertown, Duxbury, Mass., 201
Tin Peddlers' Path, Rexford, N.Y., 200
tinplate, from Britain, 76
  making of, 13
  price of in 1815, 115, 116
  size of, 13
Tinsmith's Locks, Honesdale, Pa., 200-201
Thatcher, Oxenbridge (merchant), 39
Thetford, Vt., 135
Thomas, Sidney (peddler), 101
Thompson, Dr. Harold W., 18
Thompsontown, Pa., 156
Thomson, William (smith), 158
tôle ware, 203, 209-210
toolmakers, 64, 65-68
tools, tinsmith's 14-15, 37, 38, 39, 42, 43, 65, 107, 137
top hats, of tin, 25, 27
toy, jointed, 26, 26
Tracy Brothers (tinmen), 97, 188
trade signs, 21
Travels in New England and New York, 56-57

trays, 13, 77, 162
  Butler, 127, 129, 132, 134
  coffin-lid, 101, 105, 113, 162
  North, 138
  Pennsylvania, 151, 154
  Shaker, 120
Treatise on Domestic Economy, A, 23
treatment of apprentices, 52-53
trinket box, 142
Troy, N.Y., 176; see also Lansingburg
Truman, James (smith), 153
trunks, shape of, 89, 106
Tryon, George (smith), 153
tulips, on Butler ware, 129, 143
  on Pennsylvania ware, 161
Tulpehocken Brook, Pa., 150
Turkey Valley, Pa., 149
turpentine, for japanning, 117

Uebele, M. (tinman), 161
Unadilla, N.Y., 186
unpainted tinware, 12; see also Shaker ware
Upson, Salmon (tinman), 81
Upson, Sarah Manning (decorator), 81, 84
Upson family, James (tinmen), 61
utensils, 12, 23, 24-25
Uxbridge, Mass., 172

vane, see weathervane
Veeder, Abe (tin museum), 11
Verbeek, Jan, estate of, 12
Vrooman, John (collector), 74

wagon, see carts
Wales, ware from, 209
Walker, —— (tinman), 172
Walsh, Alexander (storekeeper), 120
Wapping, Conn., 92, 157
Warner, Frank (tinker), 182
Washington, George, 180
Watervliet, N.Y., 112-113
Watts, Mrs. J. B., 97
weathervanes, 26, 36, 40
Webb, Wheaton P. (author), 192
wedding certificate, tin, 27
Wells, Milo (peddler), 100
Wells sisters (Shakers), 124
Werner, William (tinman), 66
Westbrook, Me., see Stevens Plains
West Fort Ann, N.Y., 185
West Hartwick, N.Y., 63

Westport, N.Y., 177
wet-on-wet blending of colors, 145
Weygandt, Cornelius (author), 167
whale-oil lamps, 30, 31
whirligigs, 28
Whitbeck, Mrs. Theodore (collector), 17, 130, 132, 133
White, William (collector), 28
Whiting, Calvin (smith), 43-46, 77
Whiting, Hallam (signature), 83
Whittier, John Greenleaf, 46
wholesale trade, 153, 170-171
Wilcox, Benjamin (tinman), 98
"Will" (writer on peddlers), 95-96
Willard, Emma (poet), 57
Williams, Abigail (decorator), 82
Williams, Hiram (peddler), 196-197
Williams, Samuel (smith), 153
willow tree, on punched ware, 162
Wilson, "Honest" (peddler), 145, 189
Windsor, Conn., 63, 79
Wingahocking River, 148
Winterthur Museum, H. F. Du Pont, 147, 149, 151, 154, 155, 160, 161, 162, 169, 187, 195
Winthrop, John, 13
wire, for edges of utensils, 14, 117
Wood, Warren (murderer), 196-197
Woodford, Chauncey, Ebenezer, and Isaiah (comb-makers), 93
Woodstock, Conn., 22, 158
wool, as barter, 97
Wordsworth, William, 69
workers, in Shaker shops, 126
Wray Stephen Van Renselaer (peddler), 70, 120
wriggling, decoration, 159, 160, 161, 164
Wright, Dan (smith), 59
Wright, Malcolm (smith), 153
Wyoming County, N.Y., 73

Yale, Burrage (tinman), 68
Yale, Vivian B. (peddler), 46, 119
York, Duke of, on apprentices, 52, 53